a LEISURE-PLAN book in colour

cooking for your freezer

AUDREY ELLIS

contents

Research Editor Jennie Reekie

Leisure-Plan books in colour are for pleasure and better living—the special kind of pleasure which comes from success with a rewarding hobby or pastime, or a more expert knowledge of home crafts.
   Authoritative, lively, packed with up-to-date information, these books can be built into a library for the whole family.

HAMLYN
London·New York·Sydney·Toronto

Pictured on front cover: Rich beef stew (see page 30)
Pictured on back cover: Lamb cutlets in pastry (see page 40)

introduction

A new dimension has been added to refrigeration by the growing popularity of home freezers. Any housewife who invests in a freezer will soon find that she is making considerable savings in those two precious commodities, time and money. Just how much time and money can be saved is often surprising, since we are not yet sufficiently freezer-conscious in this country to appreciate fully what a useful piece of equipment it is.

In fact the decision to buy a freezer is often taken simply because the frozen-food compartment of the refrigerator has become too small for the family needs. At first you may tend to think of your freezer only as a welcome extension of storage space for those invaluable packets of peas and fish fingers, but it is really much more than that. Certainly it does allow you to buy commercially frozen food in bulk and thus save money, but it also makes it possible for you to buy fresh foods in large quantities more cheaply, and freeze them yourself.

There is a growing trend towards discount shopping with refrigerated vans delivering a large order of frozen food, possibly only once a month, direct to your door. Purchasers can take advantage of a scheme whereby the freezer is offered at a special price, complete with a free stock of food equivalent to about one-third of its cost, by enterprising firms who will then have a regular customer for their bulk-frozen foods. Savings in housekeeping expenses when shopping is done this way are, over the period of about a year, quite dramatic.

It is also extremely economical and satisfying to preserve the produce of your own garden for use all the year round. If you are a town-dweller and cannot grow your own fruit and vegetables, you may be one of those astute shoppers who buy such foods for freezing when a seasonal glut brings down the price in the shops. So far, so good. You are saving money on

your housekeeping and a great deal of valuable time because your shopping sprees are far less frequent. However, this does not by any means exploit the potential of your freezer to the full. One of its most important uses, not yet fully appreciated by freezer owners, is for the storage of home-cooked food.

Cooking for the freezer is tremendously rewarding, in all sorts of ways. For instance, making the most of seasonal delights. If you grow raspberries, resist the temptation to eat them all at once with cream and sugar. Freeze some just as they are, for winter treats, but also make some raspberry ice-cream and sorbets for "special occasion" meals at the same time. The June crop of young peas freezes well for a fresh vegetable all the year round, and the tougher peas make a marvellous soup for freezing.

However, the freezer really comes into its own when you begin to experiment with cooking in larger quantities than usual and freezing made-up dishes for future use. The scope here is extremely wide—soups, sauces, main meals, puddings, bread, cakes, sandwiches and pastry. Almost every item you would normally prepare and cook just in advance of the meal for which it was needed can be made and stored in the freezer.

To the busy housewife, ownership of a freezer can open up a new era of easy meal-planning and preparation. You can cook at the time of day that suits you; perhaps during a quiet couple of hours in the afternoon. Besides having one meal ready to serve the same day, you can reduce repetitive kitchen chores to the minimum by planning ahead of your requirements and cooking in larger quantities then freezing several meal-sized portions. Later in the book you will see exactly how much time and effort can be saved at the busiest periods of the day and how much more varied the menus you can offer your family will be.

Maybe you have bought a freezer, and your first reaction on seeing it installed and ready for use has been, "How can I best fill all that space?" Or perhaps you are still only thinking of investing in a freezer, and wondering whether it would really be as invaluable as you hope. In either case this book is for you. There are books which are devoted mainly to the principles of freezing and preparing food for freezing, with only a section on cooking for the freezer, and a list of these is given on page 80. If your freezer did not come complete with a comprehensive instruction booklet on the subject, you will probably want to own one or more of these books. But here we are going to give minimum space to the rules for successful freezing and maximum space to recipes for dishes that freeze and defrost successfully.

There are many claims made about which foods will freeze well, and which will not. The criterion is always whether the food tastes delicious when defrosted and served—or disappointing. But the only conclusion which I and my research editor Jennie Reekie have formed is that you cannot be too enterprising. Test, adapt if you wish, and taste for yourself, so that you build up your own repertoire of favourite freezer recipes.

some useful facts and figures

Comparison of weights and measures

English weights and measures have been used throughout this book. 3 teaspoons equal 1 tablespoon. The average English teacup holds $\frac{1}{4}$ pint or 1 gill. The average English breakfast cup holds $\frac{1}{2}$ pint or 2 gills.

When cups are mentioned in recipes they refer to a B.S.I. measuring cup which holds $\frac{1}{2}$ pint or 10 fluid ounces. Three B.S.I. standard tablespoons equal approximately 2 fluid ounces.

In case it is wished to translate any of the weights and measures into their American or metric counterparts, the following notes and table give a comparison.

Liquid measure

The most important difference to be noted is that the American pint is 16 fluid ounces, as opposed to the British Imperial pint and Australian and Canadian pints which are 20 fluid ounces. The American $\frac{1}{2}$-pint measuring cup is equivalent to two-fifths of a British pint. A British $\frac{1}{2}$ pint (10 fluid ounces) is equal to $1\frac{1}{4}$ U.S. cups.

Metric weights and measures

It is difficult to convert to metric measures with absolute accuracy, but 1 oz. is equal to approximately 30 grammes, 1 lb. is equal to approximately 450 grammes, 2 lb. 3 oz. to 1 kilogramme. For liquid measure, approximately $1\frac{3}{4}$ British pints (35 fluid ounces) may be regarded as equal to 1 litre; 1 demilitre is half a litre ($17\frac{1}{2}$ fluid ounces), and 1 decilitre is one-tenth of a litre ($3\frac{1}{2}$ fluid ounces).

Solid measure

British	American
1 lb. butter or other fat	2 cups
1 lb. flour	4 cups
1 lb. granulated or castor sugar	2 cups
1 lb. icing or confectioners' sugar	3 cups
1 lb. brown (moist) sugar	$2\frac{1}{2}$ cups
1 lb. golden syrup or treacle	1 cup
1 lb. rice	2 cups
1 lb. dried fruit	2 cups
1 lb. chopped meat (firmly packed)	2 cups
1 lb. lentils or split peas	2 cups
1 lb. coffee (unground)	$2\frac{1}{4}$ cups
1 lb. soft breadcrumbs	4 cups
$\frac{1}{2}$ oz. flour	1 level tablespoon
1 oz. flour	1 heaped tablespoon
1 oz. sugar	1 level tablespoon
$\frac{1}{2}$ oz. butter	1 level tablespoon smoothed off
1 oz. golden syrup or treacle	1 level tablespoon
1 oz. jam or jelly	1 level tablespoon

All U.S. standard measuring tablespoons.

British tablespoon and ounce equivalents

Note: These measurements are approximate, and therefore must not be used for larger quantities than 2 oz. The B.S.I. tablespoon measure has been used and all tablespoon measures are level.

Commodity	Tablespoons	Ounces
Sugars		
castor sugar	2	1 oz.
demerara sugar	2	1 oz.
granulated sugar	2	1 oz.
icing sugar	4	1 oz.
soft brown sugar	3	1 oz.
Syrups		
golden syrup	1	1 oz.
honey	1	1 oz.
treacle	1	$\frac{3}{4}$ oz.
Nuts		
ground almonds	3	1 oz.
18 whole almonds	–	1 oz.
chopped hazelnuts	3	1 oz.

Commodity	Tablespoons	Ounces	Commodity	Tablespoons	Ounces
whole hazelnuts	2	1 oz.	curry powder	4	1 oz.
whole pistachios	2	1 oz.	flour	3	1 oz.
chopped walnuts	3	1 oz.	rice	2	1 oz.
8 walnut halves	—	1 oz.			

Crumbs

Commodity	Tablespoons	Ounces
dried breadcrumbs	6	1 oz.
fresh breadcrumbs	7	1 oz.
packet crumbs	4	1 oz.

Dried fruit

Commodity	Tablespoons	Ounces
currants	2	1 oz.
8 glacé cherries	—	1 oz.
cut peel	1	1 oz.
seedless raisins	2	1 oz.
sultanas	2	1 oz.

Miscellaneous

Commodity	Tablespoons	Ounces
arrowroot	2	1 oz.
cocoa powder	3	1 oz.
desiccated coconut	4	1 oz.
ground coffee	4	1 oz.
instant coffee	7	1 oz.
cornflour	2	1 oz.

Oven temperatures

Description	Electric Setting	Gas Mark
very cool	225 °F	$\frac{1}{4}$
	250 °F	$\frac{1}{2}$
cool	275 °F	1
	300 °F	2
moderate	325 °F	3
	350 °F	4
moderately hot	375 °F	5
	400 °F	6
hot	425 °F	7
	450 °F	8
very hot	475 °F	9

Note: This table is an approximate guide only.

Paella (see page 34)

how freezing works

Freezing is nature's own way of preserving food. The Romans used it in their famous underground ice-rooms, and they were certainly not the first. It is simple, safe and completely reliable. There is no need to fear that mysterious moulds, fermentation or discoloration will occur as it sometimes does when you bottle fruit or make jam. Wrap the food carefully, freeze quickly, and store just below 0°F., and you can be sure it will come out of the freezer when you want it in perfect condition months or even a year later – in some cases it could be years later.

No magic is involved. The growth of bacteria and other organisms which spoil food can only take place within a limited temperature range, around blood heat. Reduce the temperature of food well below that range, and all harmful activity ceases. However, any bacteria present when the food is frozen are not destroyed, merely dormant; they will wake up ready to multiply as soon as the food is thawed out and again reaches the temperature zone of bacterial activity.

That is why it is important to choose food for freezing which is really fresh. Keep it perfectly clean and handle as little as possible, and then freeze quickly, so that it contains as few harmful organisms as possible. The ideal way is to take the food down to several degrees below 0°F. with 24 hours; 5°F. below zero is the desirable temperature for long-term storage.

Quick freezing is important for another reason. Slow freezing allows large ice crystals to form and causes a breakdown of the food fibres. This means that food frozen more slowly tends to be flabby and discoloured when thawed out.

Choosing a freezer
The choice of the type and size of freezer suitable for your particular needs depends on several factors. If you have room in your kitchen to accommodate another fairly large piece of equipment, the chest freezer (opening from the top) is probably the most useful and economical choice. The top may be used as a work surface or, if not intended for the purpose, easily be covered with a removable work top. Since there is very little loss of cold air when this type of freezer is opened, the running cost per cubic foot of storage space is extremely reasonable.

If you do not have the floor space to spare which one of the larger chest freezers would occupy, there is the English Electric chest which is square and only requires 21 square inches of floor space. For housewives who dislike the idea of bending down to reach into a chest freezer and lifting out heavy baskets, there are many front-opening models which almost resemble a refrigerator in appearance. In fact, if space is really limited, you cannot do better than invest in a freezer-fridge. With this piece of equipment, the freezer is designed as either the upper or the lower section of a tall refrigerator, giving you two entirely different units on the same basic floor area, each with its own separate door. Loss of cold air from this type of freezer is considerably greater. If you are unable to resist the temptation to open the freezer frequently, and it is sited in a warm kitchen, the running costs may be appreciably higher.

It is always worthwhile taking the advice of an expert on the best position for your freezer. A refrigeration engineer will certainly recommend a well-ventilated area of the kitchen, even if it is nearer the cooker and therefore warmer, than a cold area with poor ventilation. He may also advise you that an old-fashioned larder, garage or out-house is a more suitable site than your kitchen and this may be more helpful to you if floor space is limited. Be sure too, that you get professional advice on the suitability of the socket and the plug you intend to use, and the correct voltage.

The size of freezer you choose should really be governed by the number of people for whom you have to cater. But here are a few facts which may help you in your choice.

1 Domestic deep freezers are available from approximately 1½ cubic feet capacity up to 20 cubic feet.
2 Each cubic foot stores about 25 lb. of frozen food.
3 If you intend to make considerable use of the freezer other than as additional storing space for commercially frozen foods, you should allow 2 cubic feet per person per week.
4 A freezer uses about 1½ units of electricity per cubic foot per week.

The most popular sizes at the lower end of the range are 1¾ cubic feet, 4 cubic feet, 6 cubic feet and 9 cubic feet. A good choice of models is available in this size range currently priced between £45 and £90.

By taking advantage of special discount terms, or buying a particular model which has just been discontinued, it is often possible to buy a new freezer for very much less than the prices quoted above.

If you are uncertain whether or not to invest such a large sum in a freezer, you may consider buying a second-hand reconditioned ice-cream conservator (which is really a chest-type freezer). These are available with a reasonable guarantee from dealers, at prices ranging upwards from £20. They may not always have a long life, but within this period you will probably have saved more than the initial cost of the freezer and will have had an opportunity to decide whether it has become a necessary part of your household equipment.

WHY YOU NEED A FREEZER

Most freezer owners, although their individual needs may be very different, agree that their freezer saves time and money in catering. If you belong to any of the following categories you will soon find your freezer so useful you will wonder how you ever managed without it:

Bachelors of both sexes. Shopping is often a problem for working girls or independent males who live alone but like to do their own cooking. The freezer can be stocked up once a month with frozen foods and one big weekend cooking spree will probably suffice to vary the contents with a number of made-up dishes. Instead of making a big stew and eating a little of it every evening for almost a week, you can cook a different dish in a large quantity every weekend and freeze a number of portions. Then you will always have a choice of main dishes to hand.

Sandwich-making can be coped with in the same way. Make up a big batch every few weeks, so that you need only take your daily ration of assorted sandwiches from the freezer each morning just as you are leaving for work.

Considerable savings can be made by buying large family-size packs of frozen food rather than the proportionately more expensive small portions to be eaten on the day of purchase. The same problems are often experienced by two bachelors, or two business girls sharing a flat who are away from home all day and of course by married couples as well, where both partners are working full-time.

Town-dwelling housewife. It may be relatively easy for her to go down to the shops every day if need be, but the great saving here is in time spent cooking. Money can be saved too by scouting around the supermarkets to take advantage of special low-price offers, catering packs and so on. It is a great convenience for the housewife to leave meals ready for the family in the freezer when she wants to go out for the day or if one member of the family always has to eat at different hours from the rest. This is often the case with large families where some children are still at home all day, and others are at school or even out at work.

Country-dwelling housewife. The housewife who lives some distance from a town finds the freezer invaluable in saving her long tedious journeys to the nearest shopping centre. Travelling costs are frequently high, public transport may be erratic, and if she drives herself, there may be parking difficulties while shopping.

Almost certainly she has her own garden crops and the offer of free produce from friends who may also have a seasonal glut. This provides a golden opportunity to stock the freezer with free food which in a few months' time would be extremely expensive to buy when the fresh fruit and vegetables concerned are out of season.

Garden-owning housewife. It is surprising how much one can grow in the way of freeze-worthy fruit and vegetables on the smallest plot of ground, and how much money this saves. Most gardeners have experienced the embarrassment of not knowing what to do with an enormous quantity of, for example, Brussels sprouts, when the season has been favourable for them. Freeze some and produce them at a time when fresh sprouts are not available.

Elderly people. An older person living alone or a retired couple encounter special problems in catering. The time-saving factor may not be so important here, but shopping in bad weather and carrying home heavy baskets can be an ordeal. Many arduous shopping expeditions can be saved if there is a well-stocked freezer in the home. Often kind relatives or friends may offer to come in and combine paying a visit with cooking a meal. It is most useful if sufficient is prepared to allow some portions to be frozen for future use. A freezer is a wonderful Silver Wedding present or retirement gift.

Centigrade	Fahrenheit	
7°	47°	Average temperature in main
4°	40°	cabinet of refrigerator
0°	32°	Freezing point of water
-6°	21°	Temperature of frozen food storage compartment in refrigerator ★
-12°	10°	Temperature of frozen food storage compartment in refrigerator ★★
-18°	0°	Temperature of frozen food storage compartment in refrigerator ★★★
-18°	0°	Deep freezers (storing food)
-21°	-5°	Deep freezers
-24°	-12°	(freezing fresh food)
-34°	-30°	Temperature at which foods are quick-frozen commercially

Temperatures for food preservation

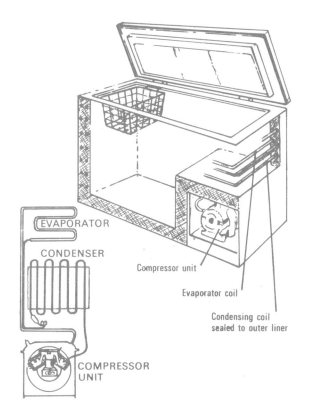

How your freezer works

A special cooling liquid circulates through the compressor, condenser and evaporator, alternately being heated by absorption of heat from the freezer and being super-cooled ready to absorb more heat.

how to prepare food for freezing

The first step is to ensure that you understand how your freezer works and how to regulate it. In most cases you will be able to reduce the temperature so that you can "freeze-down" food as quickly as possible. Remember to reduce the temperature 2 or 3 hours before adding unfrozen food. Once a new batch of food is completely frozen, you can restore the normal temperature which should be in the range between 0°F. and minus 5°F.

THE GOLDEN RULES

You will find food that has been carefully prepared for freezing will repay the little extra trouble taken, by its excellent appearance and flavour when thawed out. However, I must emphasise that it is very easy and quick to prepare food the right way and that no costly materials or elaborate techniques are required.

1 All food to be frozen should be of prime quality and in perfect condition. Do not attempt to freeze over-ripe or bruised fruit, and especially not cooked dishes unless you are certain they are completely fresh.

2 Freeze food as soon as possible after you have bought or picked it. Remember that the longer the time lag, the greater the possibility of food becoming contaminated by bacteria or deteriorating from the natural processes which continue until both bacterial activity and deterioration are arrested by the process of freezing.

3 Cooked foods must be cooled before placing in the freezer, otherwise the temperature inside the cabinet will be disturbed. Since bacterial growth is at its most active in hot or tepid food, it is a wise safety precaution to cool cooked foods as rapidly as possible until they reach a low enough temperature to put them into the freezer. Vegetables or fruit which have been blanched can be cooled in cold or iced water. Cooked dishes can often be boxed, bagged, or completely sealed in a foil wrapping and the container plunged into cold water (see page 30).

4 Use boxes, bags or wrapping material which you know to be moisture-vapour-proof. The easiest and cheapest materials to use are plastic boxes with well-fitting lids, polythene bags, clean cream and yoghourt cartons and heavy-duty aluminium foil.

5 Wash your hands before handling food for freezing, make sure that any utensils you use are perfectly clean and boxes which have been used before are carefully washed.

6 Having frozen the food successfully, remember to use it in rotation so that certain packs are not forgotten while other newer ones are used. Follow the directions given for thawing carefully to ensure the best results (see below).

FOODS UNSUITABLE FOR FREEZING

Certain foods are unsuitable for freezing and so avoid trying to freeze them, or you may be disappointed. These foods include: cooked eggs, mayonnaise, cucumber, melon, all salad greens, jellies, whole bananas, cooked new potatoes. However, experiment will soon show you whether any doubtful items freeze well.

THAWING OUT FOR USE

Most fruits require 6–8 hours to thaw in the refrigerator, 2–4 hours at room temperature. Blanched vegetables are cooked from the frozen state so do not require thawing. Most fish, shellfish, meat, poultry and game require overnight thawing in the refrigerator, or for 3–6 hours at

If kitchen space is limited, then a freezer fridge is the best choice (see page 5)

AWARDED SILVER CHALLENGE CUP ROYAL INTERNATIONAL DAIRY SHOW

VEAL AND HAM
PIE

HERBY
BEEF
LOAF

room temperature according to size, and in fact large joints and birds need up to 48 hours. Baked foods take from 15 minutes to 2 hours at room temperature according to size. Remember that, for convenience, some pastry and biscuits can be frozen in the uncooked state and put straight in the oven while still frozen.

PACKING MATERIALS

Some materials are expensive to buy, but may be used over and over again and are therefore cheaper in the end. Here is a list of different types of wrappings which are suitable.

Aluminium foil. This is one of the most suitable and versatile wrappings because it makes completely airtight parcels or can be moulded into the desired shape. Ideally, use heavy-duty foil but a thinner foil, if used double thickness, is also successful. For example, semi-liquid foods such as a stew can be cooked in a saucepan lined with foil and completely sealed into a parcel in the foil, then frozen in the correct shape for reheating in the same saucepan. You can also buy foil dishes in the shape of pudding basins, pie dishes, flan cases, and so on. These are particularly useful for small or individual portions.

Plastic containers. These, unlike aluminium foil, need not be discarded after use and if carefully washed can be used repeatedly. The best containers are semi-rigid with really well-fitting lids which give a completely airtight seal. They are recommended for fruit, vegetables, sauces, ice-cream and cooked made-up dishes such as stuffed cabbage rolls.

Polythene bags. These are probably the cheapest and easiest wrappings for frozen food. Providing there are no sharp edges on the food (such as on meat or chicken joints) which tend to pierce holes, heavy-duty bags are suitable for almost any food and an airtight seal can be made with plastic-coated wires. Only the bag need be thrown away after use, the closures can be used again.

Waxed cartons. Both round and square waxed cartons are sold specially for freezing, the round ones with screw top lids to make a seal. These can sometimes be used again once or even twice if treated carefully. However, discarded cream and yoghourt cartons are quite suitable provided they are clean and undamaged; the top can be covered with a moulded lid of foil to make a firm seal.

Plastic sheet. Rolls of plastic sheet may be used to wrap bulky or awkwardly shaped parcels, using either the butcher's wrap or druggist's wrap method (see page 11). It is useful for joints of meat, whole chickens, bread or cakes and needs to be sealed with special freezer tape. Ordinary self-adhesive tape tends to crack when reduced to a very low temperature. A type of self-adhesive plastic film can be used without any other sealing being necessary, but it is very thin and quite fragile.

Over-wrapping. Since all wrapping materials tend to crack at low temperatures, any parcel which is an awkward shape should be over-wrapped to prevent puncturing of other parcels. Stockinette or brown paper can be used for suitably shaped parcels. Old, clean, nylon stockings can also be used.

HEADSPACES

It is necessary when packing food with a high water content for freezing to leave a space between food and container lid. This allows for the expansion caused by freezing the food in sub-zero temperatures. About $\frac{1}{2}$-inch space should be left for 1-pint size dry packs and $\frac{3}{4}$–1 inch for wet packs in narrow topped containers. A wider topped container needs $\frac{1}{2}$–1 inch. When using containers which are larger than pint-size, double headspace is needed.

SEALING AND LABELLING

Close-fitting, snap-on plastic lids or waxed cartons with screw-tops or press-on lids require no further sealing. Heavy-duty foil also makes a perfect seal if firmly folded. Bags should be sealed with a twist of plastic-coated wire and other parcels with freezer tape.

Use a wax crayon for marking labels as ink, ordinary pencil or ball-point pen may fade or run. Self-adhesive stick-on labels or tie-on luggage labels are both suitable.

METHODS OF PACKING

Vegetables and fruit are usually packed in waxed cartons, plastic boxes or polythene bags. Vegetables which are to be eaten cooked freeze well but require blanching before packing. Salad vegetables, because of their high water content, are unsuitable for freezing. Fruit is usually packed raw, with or without sugar.

Fuller information on the process of blanching vegetables will be found in books dealing with freezing techniques, but the general principle is to plunge the vegetables into boiling water for a few minutes, drain and chill in iced water or in running cold water as quickly as possible and then pack at once. This process of blanching destroys enzyme activity which causes deterioration of the vegetable.

Fruit with a firm skin can be packed dry, but soft, juicy fruits are better packed with layers of sugar. Fruits which discolour easily can be packed in syrup. A medium strength is 40 per cent syrup made with 11 oz. sugar and 1 pint water.

When packing fruit in syrup or any other food with a high liquid content, it is necessary to leave about 1-inch headspace beneath the lid. This is because water expands on freezing and if no space is left, the pack will burst.

Meat, poultry and other bulky items (such as bread and cakes) are usually wrapped into parcels by the popular "butcher's wrap" method, where the food is placed in the corner of the paper or foil and the corner folded over the food and the two sides folded across the top. Roll the package over and fasten with freezer tape. Another way of packaging is the "druggist's wrap" method where the food is placed in the centre of the paper or foil and the longer edges are brought together and folded until the paper or foil is wrapped tightly against the food. Fold in the short ends and seal all edges with tape. Parcels with sharp corners are best over-wrapped for added protection. Close wrapping to exclude all air is desirable. Cooked foods, if they are solid, are usually parcelled or packed in foil trays or bags. Liquid foods such as stews are packed in boxes, or frozen until sufficiently solid to cut into portions and wrapped. They may also be frozen in the foil used to line the cooking utensil, or poured into polythene bags inside a container to give the shape, and removed from container after freezing, leaving the food in a convenient shape for packing, and in some cases, reheating. *Do not forget to exclude all air from wrapped packs or to allow headspace for expansion of liquids on freezing.*

A great deal remains to be said on packing materials and techniques, which is more fully explained in books devoted to the subject of freezing generally (see list on page 80).

Above left: Place prepared foil dividers between each chop so that they can be easily separated when taken out of the freezer.

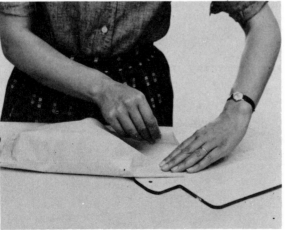

Above right: Transfer the chops to the centre of a piece of moisture-vapour-proof paper, cut large enough to provide a good overlap down the centre and at each end.

Left: Use the druggist's method of wrapping and fold the end pieces neatly to help to ensure a good seal.

bonus cooking

It is easy to see the advantages of preparing a particularly delicious but rather elaborate dish in quantity, and freezing two or more portions for further use. But the bonus of freezing cooked food is in fact a far bigger one than this.

For instance, many "made-up" dishes require the addition of a basic sauce. To obtain the greatest variety for the least effort, try making a large batch of basic sauce. Freeze some to use with left-overs or to add interest to convenience foods. But, at the same time, make up several of those dishes which use the sauce as part of their ingredients.

Béchamel, for instance, the classic savoury white sauce, is needed for Tuna Pie (see recipe on page 16), Mushroom Vol-au-vent Filling (page 17) and a dish of Sweetbreads in Cream Sauce (page 16). The portion you freeze "straight" can be used to mask freshly hard-boiled eggs (or not quite hard-boiled, as the French like them), to make a splendid light lunch or supper.

How often have you thumbed through a recipe book and decided with regret—probably because of pressure of time—not to attempt a certain recipe because it required a quantity of Béchamel?

Saucemaking is a time-consuming job. Professional chefs who suggest some recipes as being simple, tend to forget that the housewife does not have basic white and brown sauces always to hand, as he probably has in his kitchen.

As for family cakes, the time wasted in baking a three-egg Victoria Sandwich once a week will be

From top to bottom
Lasagne al forno (see page 15)
Stuffed cabbage leaves (see page 15)
Spaghetti Bolognese (see page 15)

a thing of the past when you become accustomed to bake and freeze a month's supply of cakes.

Rich tomato sauce

* When cooked, freeze $1\frac{1}{2}$ pints in $\frac{1}{2}$ pint containers for serving with fish, minced beef, rissoles and vegetables, or use as a base for meat sauces.
* Use $\frac{1}{2}$ pint to make Tomato Soup (see page 14).
* Use $\frac{1}{2}$ pint to make Plaice Provençal (see page 14).
* Use $\frac{1}{2}$ pint to make Meat Balls in Tomato Sauce (see page 14).

Pre-cooking time   30 minutes

You will need for 3 pints basic sauce:

$4\frac{1}{2}$ oz. butter	3 pints water
3 large onions, finely chopped	3 beef stock cubes
3 cloves garlic, pressed or very finely chopped	3 teaspoons dried mixed herbs
$4\frac{1}{2}$ oz. flour	3 teaspoons sugar
3 cans tomato purée (5 oz. size)	2 bay leaves
	salt and pepper

Melt butter in a large pan and fry onion and garlic until golden. Stir in flour and cook over a gentle heat until golden. Stir in tomato purée, then gradually add water.

Bring to the boil, stirring all the time until mixture bubbles and thickens. Add stock cubes, herbs, sugar, bay leaves and seasoning. Cover and simmer gently for 25 minutes. Remove bay leaves.

To freeze 1 pint basic sauce: Pour into two $\frac{1}{2}$ pint plastic or other suitable containers, leaving $\frac{1}{2}$-inch headspace. Cool quickly, seal and freeze.

To serve: Allow to thaw at room temperature for 4 hours. Reheat gently, beating from time to time. If necessary, add a little extra water.

Meat balls in tomato sauce

Tomato soup

You will need for 4 servings:
1 can tomato juice   ½ pint basic rich tomato
   (14 fl. oz. size)   sauce (see page 13)
½ pint milk

Add tomato juice and milk to sauce. Mix together and season to taste.
To freeze: Pour into plastic or other suitable container, leaving ½-inch headspace. Seal and freeze.
To serve: Allow to thaw at room temperature for 6 hours and reheat gently, or reheat very gently while still frozen.

Plaice Provençal

Pre-cooking time   10 minutes
Cooking time and oven temperature, when serving
20 minutes at 350°F., Gas Mark 4

You will need for 4 servings:
8 fillets plaice, skinned   1 small green pepper,
salt and pepper   cut in strips
1 oz. butter, melted   ½ pint rich tomato sauce
                    (see page 13)

Season fillets of plaice with salt and pepper and roll up, starting from the head end. Brush with melted butter and grill until just cooked.

Plunge pepper strips into boiling water for 2 minutes. Drain and add to sauce.
To freeze: Pack plaice rolls into a foil dish or other suitable container. Pour over tomato sauce. Cool quickly, seal and freeze.
To serve: Allow to thaw at room temperature for 6 hours. Reheat gently in a moderate oven for 20 minutes.

Meat balls in tomato sauce

Pre-cooking time   15 minutes
Cooking time and oven temperature, when serving
20 minutes at 350°F., Gas Mark 4

You will need for 4 servings:
12 oz. lean minced beef   1 egg, beaten
4 oz. white breadcrumbs   fat for shallow frying
2 tablespoons chopped   ½ pint basic rich tomato
   parsley   sauce (see page 13)
salt and pepper

Mix beef, breadcrumbs, parsley and seasoning together and bind with egg. Form into 12 balls. Fry in shallow fat until golden, about 15 minutes.
To freeze: Pack into a plastic or other suitable container. Pour over tomato sauce, cool quickly, seal and freeze.
To serve: Allow to thaw at room temperature for 6 hours. Reheat gently in a moderate oven for 20 minutes. See photograph above.

14

Basic Bolognese sauce

When cooked divide mixture into 4 portions. Freeze 2 for serving with spaghetti or noodles for 4 people. From remaining sauce make Lasagne al Forno and Stuffed Cabbage Leaves.

1 lb. basic Bolognese sauce in recipes means using 1 lb. meat, i.e. $\frac{1}{4}$ of the quantity below.

Cooking time 1$\frac{1}{4}$ hours

You will need for 4 lb. sauce:

10 oz. streaky bacon, chopped	2 tablespoons salt
4 lb. lean minced beef	$\frac{1}{2}$ teaspoon freshly milled black pepper
6 large onions, chopped	2 teaspoons sugar
$\frac{1}{4}$ pint oil	2 cans tomato purée (5 oz. size)
1 head celery, chopped	2 pints water
5 cloves garlic, finely chopped	
1 teaspoon mixed dried herbs	

Fry bacon, beef and onions slowly in oil until brown, stirring frequently. Add remaining ingredients. Cover and simmer for 1 hour.

To freeze 2 lb. basic sauce: Cool quickly. Pour into two plastic or other suitable containers leaving $\frac{1}{2}$-inch headspace in each. Seal and freeze.

To serve sauce: Reheat very gently in saucepan while still frozen. Serve with pasta and sprinkle with Parmesan cheese if liked. See colour photograph on page 12.

Lasagne al forno

Pre-cooking time   10 minutes
Cooking time and oven temperature, when serving
1 hour at 350°F., Gas Mark 4

You will need for 4 servings:

4 pints water	1 pint Béchamel sauce (see right)
2 teaspoons oil	4 oz. Gruyère or Emmenthal cheese, grated
2 teaspoons salt	
8 oz. green or white lasagne	1 oz. Parmesan cheese, grated
1 lb. basic Bolognese sauce (see above)	

Bring water to the boil with oil and salt. Carefully put in lasagne a piece at a time and boil for 8 minutes. Drain in a colander and refresh in cold water. Place on a clean, damp tea towel to dry.

To freeze: Place half the Bolognese sauce in a 4 pint casserole, top with half the lasagne, then half the Béchamel sauce and all the Gruyère or Emmenthal cheese. Repeat layers of Bolognese sauce, lasagne and Béchamel and sprinkle with Parmesan cheese. Cover with double thickness foil or moisture-vapour-proof paper. Seal and freeze.

To serve: Reheat in a moderate oven while still frozen for 1 hour or until top is golden and mixture is hot. See colour photograph on page 12.

Stuffed cabbage leaves

Pre-cooking time   5 minutes
Cooking time and oven temperature, when serving
1$\frac{1}{2}$ hours at 350°F., Gas Mark 4

You will need for 6 servings:

12 large cabbage leaves	1 lb. basic Bolognese sauce (see left)
salt	

Remove thick stalk from cabbage leaves. Cook leaves in boiling, salted water for 5 minutes or until softened, but not cooked. Drain. Place 2 tablespoons of sauce on each leaf. Turn in edges and roll up to form a parcel.

To freeze: Pack into a foil or other suitable container. Pour over any remaining sauce. Seal and freeze.

To serve: Reheat, covered, while still frozen in a moderate oven for 1$\frac{1}{2}$ hours. See colour photograph on page 12.

Basic Béchamel sauce

★ When cooked, freeze 2$\frac{1}{2}$ pints in $\frac{1}{2}$ pint containers and use for serving with meat, fish and vegetables.

★ Use $\frac{1}{2}$ pint to make Caper Sauce (see page 16).

★ Use $\frac{1}{2}$ pint to make Mustard Sauce (see page 16).

★ Use $\frac{1}{2}$ pint to make Tuna Pie (see page 16).

★ Use 1 pint to make Mushroom Vol-au-vent Filling (see page 17).

★ Use 1 pint to make Sweetbreads in Cream Sauce (see page 16).

Pre-cooking time   about 30 minutes

You will need for 6 pints basic sauce:

6 pints milk	3 onions, halved
4 bay leaves	12 oz. butter
12 peppercorns	12 oz. flour
6 blades mace	salt and pepper
3 carrots, roughly sliced	

Put milk into a large saucepan with bay leaves, peppercorns, mace, carrots and onions. Bring very slowly to the boil, draw to one side of the stove and leave for 10 minutes. Strain. Melt

15

Sweetbreads in cream sauce

butter, add flour and cook without browning for 5 minutes. Remove from heat and gradually stir in milk. Return to heat and bring to the boil, stirring all the time until sauce bubbles and thickens. Season to taste with salt and pepper.

To freeze 2½ pints basic sauce: Pour into five ½ pint plastic or other suitable containers, leaving ½-inch headspace. Cover with a circle of damp greaseproof paper and cool quickly. Seal and freeze.

To serve: Allow to thaw at room temperature for 4 hours. Remove greaseproof paper and re-heat gently, beating from time to time. If necessary, add a little extra milk.

Note: For white sauce, make as above but do not infuse the milk with the seasoning.

Variations:

Caper Sauce: Add 2–3 teaspoons drained capers to ½ pint basic sauce. Freeze and serve as above. Use for serving with fish and boiled meats.

Mustard Sauce: Blend 2 teaspoons dry mustard with 2 teaspoons vinegar and add to ½ pint basic sauce. Freeze and serve as above. Use for serving with grilled herrings and boiled salt beef.

Tuna pie

Cooking time and oven temperature, when serving 1 hour at 400°F., Gas Mark 6

You will need for 4–6 servings:

1 can tuna (7 oz. size)	8 oz. rough puff pastry
½ pint basic Béchamel	(see page 50) or
sauce (see page 15)	13 oz. packet frozen
	puff pastry

Flake tuna and mix with sauce. Roll out pastry to a 12-inch square.

To freeze: Place square of pastry on a large piece of double thickness foil on a baking tray. Put filling in the centre and damp edges of pastry. Bring points to the centre, sealing the edges to form an envelope. Knock up the edges with the back of a knife and decorate with leaves made from the trimmings. Cover pie with foil. Seal and freeze. When frozen, remove baking tray.

To serve: Uncover and place on baking tray. Brush with milk and bake for 1 hour in a moderately hot oven.

Sweetbreads in cream sauce

Pre-cooking time   about 15 minutes

You will need for 4 servings:

1 lb. lamb's sweetbreads	4 tablespoons dry sherry
1 pint basic Béchamel	(optional)
sauce (see page 15)	salt and pepper

To serve:

¼ pint single cream	watercress to garnish

Remove fat and tissue from sweetbreads. Soak in cold water for 1 hour and strain. Bring to the boil in fresh water, simmer for about 15 minutes or until tender. Strain and rinse. Add to sauce with sherry, if liked. Season to taste with salt and pepper.

To freeze: Cool quickly. Turn into a plastic or other suitable container. Seal and freeze.

To serve: Allow to thaw at room temperature for 6 hours. Reheat gently and stir in ¼ pint single cream just before serving. Garnish with watercress. Do not allow to boil after the cream has been added. See photograph left.

Mushroom vol-au-vent filling

Pre-cooking time   about 10 minutes

You will need for 4 servings:

8 oz. mushrooms, chopped	¼ teaspoon nutmeg
2 oz. butter	salt and pepper
1 pint basic Béchamel sauce (see page 15)	

To serve:
parsley to garnish

Fry mushrooms in butter until soft. Add to sauce with nutmeg. Season to taste.

To freeze: Pour into a plastic or other suitable container, leaving ½-inch headspace. Cover with a circle of damp greaseproof paper and then cool quickly. Seal and freeze.

To serve: Allow to thaw at room temperature for 5 hours. Remove greaseproof paper and reheat, beating from time to time. Pour into hot vol-au-vent cases and serve garnished with parsley.

Variations:
Omit mushrooms and add 8 oz. cooked ham, chicken or prawns.

Basic cheese sauce

★ When cooked, freeze 2 pints in ½ pint containers and use for serving with meat, fish, eggs and vegetables.
★ Use 1 pint to make Halibut Mornay (see right).
★ Use 1 pint to make Leeks au Gratin (see page 19).
★ Use 1 pint to make Cheese and Onion Potato Topped Pie (see page 19).
★ Use 1 pint to make Ham and Asparagus Savoury (see page 19).

Pre-cooking time   15 minutes

You will need for 6 pints basic sauce:

12 oz. butter	2 tablespoons made mustard
12 oz. flour	mustard
6 pints milk	salt and pepper
2 lb. 4 oz. strong Cheddar cheese, grated	

Melt butter in a large pan, add flour and cook for 5 minutes, without browning. Remove from heat and gradually stir in milk. Return to heat and bring to the boil, stirring all the time until sauce bubbles and thickens. Stir in cheese and mustard and allow cheese to melt. Season to taste.

To freeze 2 pints basic sauce: Pour into four ½ pint plastic or other suitable containers, leaving ½-inch headspace. Cover with a circle of damp greaseproof paper and cool quickly. Seal and freeze.

To serve: Allow to thaw at room temperature for 4 hours. Remove greaseproof paper and reheat gently, beating from time to time. If necessary, add a little extra milk.

Halibut mornay

Pre-cooking time   about 10 minutes
Cooking time and oven temperature, when serving
20 minutes at 400°F., Gas Mark 6

You will need for 4 servings:

1½ lb. halibut steak, cut in 4	salt and pepper
2 oz. butter	1 pint basic cheese sauce (see left)

To serve:

2 oz. breadcrumbs	2 oz. Cheddar cheese, grated

Dot halibut steaks with butter and season with salt and pepper. Grill for about 10 minutes or until fish flakes easily with a fork.

To freeze: Place fish in a foil dish or other suitable container. Add juices from grill pan to cheese sauce and pour over fish. Cool quickly. Cover closely with foil. Seal and freeze.

To serve: Allow to thaw at room temperature for 5 hours. Mix 2 oz. breadcrumbs with 2 oz. grated Cheddar cheese and sprinkle over the top. Reheat in a moderately hot oven for 20 minutes or until topping is crisp and golden.

Leeks au gratin

Pre-cooking time   about 20 minutes
Cooking time and oven temperature, when serving
20 minutes at 400°F., Gas Mark 6

You will need for 4 servings:
8 large leeks   1 pint basic cheese
salt   sauce (see page 17)

To serve:
3 oz. Cheddar cheese, grated

Remove base of leeks and top part of leaves. Make two cuts about 3 inches from the top. Wash thoroughly in cold water to remove all the dirt and grit. Cook leeks in a large pan of boiling, salted water for about 20 minutes or until tender. Drain well.
To freeze: Place leeks in a foil dish or other suitable container and pour over cheese sauce. Cool quickly and cover closely with foil. Seal and freeze.
To serve: Allow to thaw at room temperature for 5 hours. Sprinkle with 3 oz. grated Cheddar cheese and reheat in a moderately hot oven for 20 minutes or until top is crisp and golden. See photograph left.

Cheese and onion potato topped pie

Pre-cooking time   about 30 minutes
Cooking time and oven temperature, when serving
1 hour at 400°F., Gas Mark 6

You will need for 4 servings:
1 lb. onions, chopped   salt and pepper
3 oz. butter   1½ lb. potatoes, peeled
1 pint basic cheese sauce   and halved
   (see page 17)   6 tablespoons milk

Fry chopped onions in 2 oz. of the butter for about 15 minutes or until cooked, without browning. Add to cheese sauce and adjust seasoning. Cook peeled and halved potatoes in boiling, salted water until tender. Strain and mash with remaining butter and milk. Season to taste.
To freeze: Pour cheese and onion mixture into a foil dish or other suitable container. Spread potato over the top and decorate with the tip of a round-bladed knife. Cool quickly. Cover closely with foil, seal and freeze.
To serve: Remove cover. Brush with a little milk and bake in a moderately hot oven for 1 hour or until potato is golden and mixture heated through.

Leeks au gratin

Ham and asparagus savoury

Cooking time and oven temperature, when serving
20 minutes at 400°F., Gas Mark 6

You will need for 4 servings:
1 can asparagus   1 pint basic cheese sauce
   (14 oz. size)   (see page 17)
                                  8 thin slices ham

To serve:
2 oz. Cheddar cheese, grated

Drain asparagus and blend ¼ pint of the asparagus juice with the cheese sauce. Wrap slices of ham round the asparagus spears.
To freeze: Place ham and asparagus rolls in a foil dish or other suitable container. Pour over cheese sauce and cool quickly. Cover closely with foil, seal and freeze.
To serve: Allow to thaw at room temperature for 5 hours. Sprinkle with 2 oz. grated Cheddar cheese and reheat in a moderately hot oven for 20 minutes or until top is crisp and golden.

Bonus cooking using 8 chickens

★ Freeze 1 chicken whole, wrapped in a polythene bag and sealed.
★ Remove legs from 4 chickens, coat 4 legs with egg and breadcrumbs ready for frying, leave remaining 4 plain. Place in polythene bags, seal and freeze.
★ Use 2 chicken breasts and wing joints to make Ham and Chicken Pie (see page 20).
★ Use 2 chicken breasts and wing joints to make Cold Chicken Crème (see page 20).
★ Use 4 chicken breasts to make Chinese Chicken (see page 20).
★ Use 4 chicken wings to make Chicken Soup (see page 23).
★ Use 1 whole chicken to make Terrine of Chicken (see page 22).
★ Use 1 whole chicken to make Spiced Chicken Paprika (see page 23).
★ Use 1 whole chicken to make Coq au Vin (see page 24).
★ Use chicken livers to make Sicilian Risotto (see page 24).
★ Use carcasses, including bones from chickens that have been simmered, and remaining giblets to make Chicken Stock (see page 22).
★ Use well-reduced stock to freeze into cubes for gravies and sauces.
Note: Individual methods follow overleaf, so that recipes can be made up easily if not using the bonus method, but it is obviously more practical to cook the meat for the Ham and

Chicken Pie, Cold Chicken Crème, Chicken Soup and Spiced Chicken Paprika all together. Use all the ingredients and total quantity of water, but omit salt and stock for cooking wings for soup. Any excess stock can be added to the chicken stock.

Chinese chicken

Pre-cooking time   about 20 minutes
Cooking time and oven temperature, when serving
25 minutes at 350°F., Gas Mark 4

You will need for 4 servings:

2 oz. butter	1 can pineapple pieces
4 chicken breasts,	(8 oz. size)
boned and skinned	½ oz. cornflour
salt and pepper	1 chicken stock cube
1 small green pepper,	3 tablespoons vinegar
seeded and sliced	2 tablespoons soy sauce

Melt butter in a frying pan. Season chicken with salt and pepper and fry on both sides until golden, about 15 minutes. Add green pepper after 10 minutes. Meanwhile, drain pineapple and make juice up to ½ pint with water. Blend 4 tablespoons of the juice with cornflour and bring remainder to the boil with crumbled stock cube, vinegar and soy sauce. Pour over cornflour, stirring. Return to heat and bring to the boil, stirring all the time until mixture bubbles and thickens. Add pineapple pieces and season with salt and pepper.
To freeze: Pack chicken into a foil dish or other suitable container. Add pepper and pan juices to sauce and pour sauce over chicken. Cool quickly, seal and freeze.
To serve: Allow to thaw at room temperature for 6 hours and reheat, still covered, in a moderate oven for about 25 minutes, or reheat gently in a saucepan over a low heat. Serve with rice. See photograph on page 22.

Ham and chicken pie

Pre-cooking time   about 1¾ hours
Cooking time and oven temperature, when serving
about 1 hour at 400°F., Gas Mark 6

You will need for 4–6 servings:

1 small knuckle of ham,	2 oz. butter
soaked overnight	2 oz. flour
1½ pints water	salt and pepper
1 bay leaf	6 oz. short crust pastry
1 carrot	(see page 50) or
1 onion	1 packet frozen short
2 chicken breasts and wing	crust pastry
joints	(7½ oz. size)

Put knuckle into saucepan with water, bay leaf, carrot and onion. Bring to the boil and simmer covered for 1½ hours. Add chicken joints 30 minutes before the end of cooking time. Remove ham and chicken joints, take meat off the bones, and chop into ½-inch pieces. Melt butter in pan, add flour and cook for 1 minute. Remove from heat and gradually stir in 1 pint of the strained chicken and ham stock. Return to heat and bring to the boil, stirring all the time until mixture bubbles and thickens. Remove from heat, add meat, season to taste and cool. If stock is very salty, it may be necessary to add a little milk in place of some of the stock.
Roll out pastry to an oval to fit a 2½ pint pie dish. Pour in meat mixture and top with pastry, fluting the edges.
To freeze: Freeze uncovered. When frozen, place in a polythene bag or wrap in double thickness foil. Seal and return to freezer.
To serve: Brush with milk and bake while still frozen in a moderately hot oven for about 1 hour or until pastry is golden and filling heated through.

Cold chicken crème

Pre-cooking time   about 1 hour

You will need for 3–4 servings:

2 chicken breasts and	salt and pepper
wing joints	1 oz. butter
1 pint water	1 oz. flour
1 onion	grated rind and juice
1 carrot	½ lemon
4 peppercorns	4 oz. packet frozen peas,
1 bay leaf	cooked

To serve:

¼ pint single cream	strips of pimento to garnish

Put chicken into pan with water, onion, carrot, peppercorns, bay leaf, salt and pepper. Bring to the boil and simmer for about 30 minutes. Remove chicken from pan and take off the bone. Chop into ½-inch pieces. Melt butter in pan, add flour and cook for 1 minute. Remove from heat and gradually add ½ pint of the strained chicken stock. Return to heat and bring to the boil, stirring all the time until mixture bubbles and thickens. Remove from heat and stir in lemon rind and juice, peas and chicken. Season to taste.
To freeze: Cool quickly. Turn into plastic or other suitable container, leaving ½-inch head-space.
To serve: Allow to thaw at room temperature for 8 hours. Stir in ¼ pint single cream. Serve with salad and garnish with strips of pimento.

Spring lamb pie (see page 28)

Pork chops with pears and apricots (see page 36)

Terrine of chicken

Chinese chicken (see page 20)

Pre-cooking time and oven temperature
2½ hours at 350°F., Gas Mark 4

You will need for 8 servings:

1 chicken	½ teaspoon mixed dried
6 oz. pork fat	herbs
2 onions	grated rind and juice
2 cloves garlic	1 lemon
2 tablespoons chopped	1 egg, beaten
parsley	salt and freshly milled
	black pepper

Remove breast of chicken and cut into strips. Bone out remainder of chicken and mince with pork fat, onions and garlic. Add remaining ingredients. Put half the chicken and pork mixture into a greased, straight-sided dish. Lay strips of chicken breast on top and cover with remaining chicken and pork mixture. Cover with foil and lid. Place in a roasting tin half-filled with hot water and bake in a moderate oven for 2½ hours.

To freeze: Cool quickly. Turn out of dish and wrap in double thickness foil. Seal and freeze.

To serve: Allow to thaw in refrigerator for 24 hours.

Chicken stock

Pre-cooking time   about 3 hours

You will need to every 1 lb. chicken bones and giblets:

3 pints water	1 bouquet garni
1 large carrot, sliced	1 teaspoon salt
1 large onion, quartered	pinch pepper
1 bay leaf	

Wash bones and giblets. Place in pan with remaining ingredients. Bring slowly to the boil and skim. Simmer gently for 3 hours, skimming from time to time and adding extra water as liquid evaporates. Strain through a muslin cloth and add extra seasoning to taste.

To freeze: Pour into plastic or other suitable containers, leaving 1-inch headspace. Cool quickly and skim off fat. Seal and freeze.

To prepare for use: Heat gently while still frozen or allow to thaw at room temperature for 4–6 hours, depending on quantity of stock. Use in soup, sauces and gravies.

Chicken soup

Pre-cooking time   about 30 minutes

You will need for 2–4 servings:

4 chicken wing joints	3 oz. flour
3 pints chicken stock	3 tablespoons chopped
(see page 22)	parsley
3 oz. butter	salt and pepper

To serve:

¼ pint single cream	chopped parsley

Cook chicken joints in stock for about 25 minutes. Remove from pan, take meat off the bones and chop finely. Melt butter in a pan, add flour and cook for a few minutes, without browning. Remove from heat and gradually stir in chicken stock. Return to heat and bring to the boil, stirring all the time until mixture bubbles and thickens. Remove from heat and add chicken and parsley. Season to taste.

To freeze: Cool quickly. Pour into two plastic or other suitable containers, leaving ½-inch headspace. Seal and freeze.

To serve: Allow to thaw at room temperature for 6 hours. Reheat gently and stir in ¼ pint single cream just before serving, if liked. Sprinkle with chopped parsley.

Chicken soup

Spiced chicken paprika

Pre-cooking time   about 1½ hours

You will need for 6 servings:

1 chicken	2 oz. butter
1 onion	2 oz. flour
1 blade mace	1 level tablespoon
6 peppercorns	paprika
sprig thyme	1 teaspoon made
thinly peeled rind	mustard
1 lemon	2 tablespoons redcurrant
few sprigs parsley	jelly
1 teaspoon salt	pepper
about 1½ pints water	

To serve:

¼ pint soured cream	

In a saucepan, place chicken, onion, mace, peppercorns, thyme, lemon rind, parsley, salt and water. Cover and bring to the boil; simmer until tender, about 1–1¼ hours. Remove chicken, strain stock. Take meat off the bones and cut into large pieces. Melt butter in a pan, add flour and paprika and cook for 1 minute. Remove from heat and gradually stir in 1 pint of the strained chicken stock. Return to heat and bring to the boil, stirring all the time until mixture bubbles and thickens. Stir in mustard and redcurrant

jelly. Remove from heat and stir in chicken. Season to taste.

To freeze: Cool quickly. Turn into plastic or other suitable container, leaving ½-inch headspace. Seal and freeze.

To serve: Allow to thaw at room temperature for 6 hours. Reheat gently and stir in ¼ pint soured cream just before serving. Do not allow to boil after cream has been added.

Coq au vin

Pre-cooking time and oven temperature
2 hours at 325 °F., Gas Mark 3
Cooking time and oven temperature, when serving
40 minutes at 350 °F., Gas Mark 4

You will need for 6 servings:

1 chicken	12 button or small onions
1 oz. flour	½ bottle red wine
salt and pepper	2 cloves garlic, pressed or
2 oz. butter	very finely chopped
2 tablespoons oil	2 bay leaves
4 oz. salt pork, cut in	½ teaspoon dried thyme
1-inch cubes	4 oz. button mushrooms

To serve:
chopped parsley

Cut chicken into six joints and toss in seasoned flour. Put butter and oil into a pan and fry pork and onions until golden. Remove with a draining spoon and place in a casserole. Fry chicken joints on both sides until golden. Place in casserole. Sprinkle any excess flour from chicken into fat and gradually stir in wine. Bring to the boil and pour over chicken. Add garlic, bay leaves

and thyme. Cover and place in a moderate oven for 1½ hours. Add mushrooms 15 minutes before end of cooking time. Adjust seasoning.

To freeze: Cool quickly. Turn into a plastic or other suitable container. Seal and freeze.

To serve: Allow to thaw at room temperature for 6 hours. Reheat in a moderate oven for 40 minutes. Serve sprinkled with chopped parsley.

Sicilian risotto

Pre-cooking time   25 minutes
Cooking time and oven temperature, when serving
45 minutes at 350 °F., Gas Mark 4

You will need for 4 servings:

2 tablespoons oil	4 large tomatoes,
1 large onion, chopped	peeled and chopped
8 oz. long grain rice	salt and pepper
8 chicken livers	1 tablespoon chopped
1 pint chicken stock (see	parsley
page 22) or water and	
1 chicken stock cube	

Heat oil in a pan and fry onion and rice for about 5 minutes. Add chicken livers and fry for a further 5 minutes. Stir in chicken stock. Bring to the boil, add tomatoes, cover and simmer gently for about 15 minutes or until rice is tender. Season to taste and stir in parsley.

To freeze: Cool quickly. Pack into a polythene bag or other suitable container. Seal and freeze.

To serve: Allow to thaw at room temperature for 4 hours. Place in a roasting tin, cover with foil and make a few holes in the foil with a fork

Divide basic Victoria sandwich mixture into four

Victoria sandwich—dividing mixture between two sandwich tins

Chocolate cake—spooning cake mixture into prepared tin (see page 26)

to allow the steam to escape; reheat in a moderate oven for about 45 minutes, or until heated through, stirring lightly with a fork from time to time.

Basic Victoria sandwich mixture

- ★ When prepared, divide mixture into four.
- ★ Make Victoria Sandwich (see below).
- ★ Make Queen Cakes (see right).
  Bake both these cakes together.
- ★ Make Chocolate Cake (see page 26).
- ★ Make Orange Cake (see page 26).
  Bake both these cakes together.
  Note: 6 oz. Victoria Sandwich mixture means 6 oz. butter, that is $\frac{1}{4}$ of the quantity below.

1½ lb. butter	12 eggs, beaten
1½ lb. castor sugar	1½ lb. self-raising flour

Cream butter and sugar together until light and fluffy. Gradually beat in eggs, adding a tablespoon of the sieved flour with the last amount of egg. Carefully fold in remaining flour.

Victoria sandwich

Pre-cooking time and oven temperature
20–25 minutes at 375 °F., Gas Mark 5
You will need:

6 oz. basic Victoria Sandwich mixture (see above)	3 tablespoons jam

Queen cakes—putting mixture into paper cake cases

Divide Victoria Sandwich mixture between two greased 7–8-inch sandwich tins, each lined with a circle of greaseproof paper (see photograph on page 24). Bake in a moderately hot oven for 20–25 minutes or until cakes spring back when lightly touched with tip of the finger. Turn out and cool on rack. Sandwich together with jam.
To freeze: Wrap in moisture-vapour-proof paper or double thickness foil.
To serve: Allow to thaw at room temperature for 4 hours.

Queen cakes

Pre-cooking time and oven temperature
15–20 minutes at 375 °F., Gas Mark 5
You will need:

5 oz. currants	6 oz. basic Victoria
few drops almond essence	Sandwich mixture (see left)

Fold currants and essence carefully into Victoria Sandwich mixture. Stand paper cake cases in patty tins to give cakes a good shape. Place a heaped teaspoon of the mixture into each case (see photograph above). Bake in a moderately hot oven for 15–20 minutes or until cakes spring back when lightly touched with the tip of the finger. Cool on a rack.
To freeze: Pack into a polythene bag. Seal and freeze.
To serve: Allow to thaw at room temperature for 2 hours.

Orange cake—adding grated orange rind to mixture

Chocolate cake

Pre-cooking time and oven temperature
1¼ hours at 350°F., Gas Mark 4

You will need:

1½ oz. cocoa, sieved	6 oz. basic Victoria Sandwich mixture (see page 25) about 2 tablespoons milk

Butter icing:

2 oz. cocoa	6 oz. butter
5 tablespoons boiling water	1 lb. icing sugar, sieved

Carefully fold in sieved cocoa to Victoria Sandwich mixture. Add milk so that mixture returns to its original consistency. Turn into a greased and lined 7-inch cake tin (see photograph on page 25). Bake in a moderate oven for about 1¼ hours or until mixture springs back when lightly touched with the tip of the finger. Turn out and cool on a rack. Dissolve cocoa for icing in boiling water. Cream butter and beat in icing sugar and cocoa mixture alternately. Split cake into 3 and sandwich together with some of the icing. Use remaining icing to coat top and sides of cake, and decorate with swirls using a fork.
To freeze: Place on a plate and allow icing to set. Freeze uncovered. When frozen wrap in double thickness foil or moisture-vapour-proof paper and seal. Return to the freezer.
To serve: Uncover and allow to thaw at room temperature for 4 hours.

Orange cake

Pre-cooking time and oven temperature
1¼ hours at 350°F., Gas Mark 4

You will need:

grated rind of 1 large orange	6 oz. basic Victoria Sandwich mixture (see page 25)

Orange butter icing:

2 oz. butter	1 tablespoon orange juice
4 oz. icing sugar, sieved	

Orange glacé icing:

a little orange juice	crystallised orange slices (optional)
6 oz. icing sugar, sieved	

Carefully fold orange rind into Victoria Sandwich mixture (see photograph on the left). Turn into a greased and lined 7-inch cake tin. Bake in a moderate oven for 1¼ hours or until mixture springs back when lightly touched with the tip of the finger. Turn out and cool on a rack. Cream butter and beat in icing sugar and orange juice. Split cake in half and sandwich together with the orange butter icing. Gradually beat orange juice into icing sugar to give a coating consistency. Spoon over top of cake. Decorate with crystallised orange slices if wished.
To freeze: Place on a plate and allow icing to set. Freeze uncovered. When frozen wrap in double thickness foil or moisture-vapour-proof paper and seal. Return to freezer.
To serve: Uncover and allow to thaw at room temperature for 4 hours.

main meals

A great deal of stress and strain can be avoided by cooking family meals at a time of the day to suit you—a quiet hour or so in the early afternoon, perhaps. All the recipes in this section can easily be multiplied by two or three, so that you can serve one meal on the day it is cooked and have at least one further meal to "freeze down" for the future. Most housewives who have tried this cook-ahead plan find that they can maintain a varied menu by serving one portion (large enough to feed the whole family) freshly cooked and freezing two additional portions of similar size. The cooking chores can often be reduced to one session a week by the following method.

Plan to cook at the same time two different main dishes in three-meal quantities. Serve one the same day and freeze the other two. Store one portion of the second dish in the refrigerator to re-heat the following day and freeze the other two. From one cooking session you then have two freshly cooked meals to serve and four frozen ones. Next time you have your cooking spree, you will obviously choose two other main dishes so that there should always be a selection of six or more to choose from in the freezer even if (as I strongly recommend) you restrict the freezer life of cooked dishes to one month.

Steak and kidney pie

Pre-cooking time   2 hours
Cooking time and oven temperature, when serving
1 hour at 400°F., Gas Mark 6

You will need for 4 servings:

1 lb. lean stewing steak	2 medium sized onions
6 oz. ox kidney	chopped
1 oz. flour	6 oz. puff pastry
salt and pepper	(see page 51) or
1 oz. dripping	7½ oz. packet frozen
¾ pint water	puff pastry

Cut steak into 1-inch cubes, removing fat and gristle. Remove core from kidney and cut into ½-inch pieces. Season flour well with salt and pepper and place in a polythene bag. Add meat and shake until coated with flour. Melt dripping, add onion and meat and fry for about 10 minutes, until lightly browned. Pour in water. Bring to the boil, stirring occasionally. Cover and simmer gently for 2 hours. Adjust seasoning and cool. Turn into a 2 pint pie dish or foil dish. Roll out pastry and cut out to shape of pie dish. Using trimmings, lay damp strips of pastry round the rim of the dish. Top with rolled out pastry and trim edges. Knock up the edges, using the back of a knife. Flute edges and decorate with pastry leaves, made from trimmings.
To freeze: Freeze uncovered. When frozen, wrap in double thickness foil, moisture-vapour-proof paper or a polythene bag and seal.
To serve: Brush with beaten egg or milk and bake, while still frozen, in a moderately hot oven for 1 hour or until pastry is golden and filling heated through.

Beef paprika

Pre-cooking time and oven temperature
2½ hours at 350°F., Gas Mark 4

You will need for 4–6 servings:

1½ oz. dripping	1 can tomato purée
14 small onions	(5 oz. size)
1½ lb. stewing steak	1¼ pints water
1½ oz. flour	2 beef stock cubes
salt and pepper	1 teaspoon sugar
1 level tablespoon paprika	

Melt dripping in a pan and fry onions. Cut meat into 1½-inch cubes and toss in flour, seasoned with salt, pepper and paprika. Add to pan and fry for about 10 minutes or until meat is evenly

Cassoulet

browned. Add remaining seasoned flour. Stir in tomato purée and gradually add water. Bring to the boil, stirring from time to time. Add stock cubes and sugar. Cover and simmer in a moderate oven for 2 hours or until meat is tender.

To freeze: Cool quickly. Turn into a plastic or other suitable container, leaving ½-inch headspace. Seal and freeze.

To serve: Either allow to thaw at room temperature for 6 hours and slowly reheat or reheat gently in a saucepan while still frozen, stirring from time to time.

Cassoulet

Pre-cooking time   about 4 hours
Cooking time and oven temperature, when serving
45 minutes at 375°F., Gas Mark 5

You will need for 4 servings:

8 oz. haricot beans	4 oz. lamb fillet or
1½ pints stock or water	chump chop
and stock cubes	1 can tomato purée
1 oz. lard	(2¼ oz. size)
1 large onion, chopped	1 bay leaf
2 cloves garlic, pressed or	1 teaspoon mixed herbs
finely chopped	2 oz. garlic sausage
8 oz. pickled pork	salt and pepper

To serve:
brown breadcrumbs

Soak beans overnight in cold water. Drain and place in a pan with stock. Bring to the boil, cover and simmer gently for 1 hour. Melt lard and fry onions and garlic for 5 minutes. Cut pork and lamb into ½-inch pieces and add to pan. Fry for

10 minutes. Add beans, together with stock, tomato purée, bay leaf and herbs. Cover and simmer very gently for 2½ hours. Add sliced and halved garlic sausage 30 minutes before end of cooking time. Remove bay leaf and adjust seasoning.

To freeze: Cool quickly. Pack into a plastic or other suitable container, seal and freeze.

To serve: Allow to thaw at room temperature for 8 hours. Turn into a casserole and sprinkle with brown breadcrumbs. Bake in a moderately hot oven for 45 minutes or until top is crunchy. See photograph above.

Spring lamb pie

Pre-cooking time   2 hours
Cooking time and oven temperature, when serving
about 1 hour at 400°F., Gas Mark 6

You will need for 4–6 servings:

2 pints water	1½ oz. flour
1 large carrot, peeled	4 oz. mushrooms
2 blades mace	4 oz. packet frozen peas,
2 bay leaves	cooked
2 onions, halved	pepper
6 peppercorns	6 oz. short crust pastry
2 teaspoons salt	(see page 50) or
2 lb. stewing lamb	1 packet frozen short
1½ oz. butter	crust pastry (7½ oz. size)

Put water into a large saucepan with carrot, mace, bay leaves, onions, peppercorns, salt and lamb. Bring slowly to the boil. Skim and simmer for 1½ hours. Cool and strain. Take meat off the bones and chop into ½-inch pieces. Melt butter in pan, add flour and cook for a minute. Remove from heat and gradually stir in 1 pint of strained lamb stock. Return to heat and bring to boil stirring all the time until sauce bubbles and thickens. Remove from heat and stir in lamb, mushrooms and peas. Adjust seasoning. Allow to cool. Roll out pastry to an oval to fit a 1½ pint pie dish. Pour in lamb mixture and top with pastry, fluting the edges.

To freeze: Freeze uncovered. When frozen, place in a polythene bag or wrap in double thickness foil. Seal and return to freezer.

To serve: Brush with milk and bake while still frozen in a moderately hot oven for about 1 hour or until pastry is golden and filling heated through. See colour photograph on page 21.

Veal and ham pie placed on foil

Veal and ham pie

Pre-cooking time and oven temperature
20 minutes at 400°F., Gas Mark 6 then
1 hour at 350°F., Gas Mark 4

You will need for 4–6 servings:

8 oz. pie veal	grated rind ½ lemon
6 oz. piece raw, lean bacon	4 tablespoons water
1 onion, halved	8 oz. hot water crust
salt and pepper	pastry (see page 51)
¼ teaspoon nutmeg or	1 egg, beaten
ground mace	

Mince veal, bacon and onion and mix with salt, pepper, nutmeg or mace, lemon rind and water. Using a 1 lb. loaf tin, lay one piece of double thickness foil down the length of the tin so that it overlaps at the end and lay a second piece across. Roll out two-thirds of the pastry and use to line the tin. Fill with meat mixture. Brush edges of pastry with egg and roll out remaining pastry to form a lid. Place on top of pie. Seal edges well and trim. Make a hole in the centre and decorate with pastry leaves. Bake in a moderately hot oven for 20 minutes, then lower heat to moderate and bake for a further hour. About 45 minutes before end of cooking time, lift pie carefully out of tin using the foil and place on baking tray. Brush with beaten egg and continue baking. Remove pie from baking tray and leave to cool on a rack.

Wrapping the pie in foil

To freeze: Wrap in double thickness foil or place in a polythene bag. Seal and freeze. See photographs on the right.

To serve: Allow to thaw in a refrigerator for 24 hours. After 6 hours, pour a little warm stock into the pie, using a funnel. If the stock is added at this stage, it will help the pie to defrost and the stock will form a jelly immediately.

Placing the pie in the freezer

Bigos cooked then wrapped in foil container

Cooling the Bigos in bowl of cold water

Placing labelled Bigos in freezer

Bigos

Pre-cooking time   1½ hours

You will need for 4–6 servings:

1 lb. sauerkraut	½ oz. flour
1 bay leaf	salt and pepper
1 pint water	4 oz. cooked ham,
1 lb. firm white cabbage	cut in strips
2 oz. mushrooms,	4 oz. garlic sausage or
cut in strips	salami, diced
4 oz. streaky bacon,	2 tablespoons tomato
cut in ½-inch pieces	purée
1 large onion, chopped	¼ pint red wine
8 oz. lean pork, chopped	1 clove garlic, crushed
in 1-inch pieces	

Line a large, straight-sided saucepan with thick foil, leaving plenty of foil to seal the top. Drain sauerkraut, put into the pan with bay leaf and water. Bring to the boil, simmer for 30 minutes. Meanwhile put cabbage and mushrooms into a second pan, add ½ pint water and cook as sauerkraut. Fry bacon in a separate pan until golden, remove and add to sauerkraut. Fry onion in bacon fat until golden, add to sauerkraut. Toss pork in flour seasoned with salt and pepper, fry in pan, adding a little extra fat if necessary. Add to sauerkraut and simmer for a further 45 minutes. About 30 minutes before end of cooking time add cabbage with mushrooms, ham, sausage or salami, tomato purée, wine and garlic. Season to taste.

To freeze: Seal the bigos in the foil. First bring two edges together and fold over, then fold in the ends. Stand the parcel in a bowl of cold water to cool it quickly. Label and place in the freezer. See photographs left.

To serve: Allow to thaw at room temperature for 6 hours. Reheat gently and serve with boiled potatoes.

Rich beef stew

Pre-cooking time   about 2½ hours

You will need for 4–6 servings:

2½ lb. chuck beef	3 oz. dripping
1½ oz. flour	2 tablespoons tomato
salt and pepper	purée
2 onions, chopped	1 teaspoon made mustard
2 large carrots,	1 pint brown ale
cut in rings	few sprigs parsley
1 green pepper, sliced	1 bay leaf

Cut meat into 1-inch cubes and toss in seasoned flour. Fry with onions, carrots and pepper in dripping until light brown. Remove from heat, add tomato purée and mustard, and stir in brown ale. Bring to the boil, add parsley and bay leaf. Season to taste. Simmer for $2\frac{1}{2}$ hours or until tender. Remove bay leaf.

To freeze: Cool quickly. Turn into a plastic or other suitable container, leaving $\frac{1}{2}$-inch headspace. Seal and freeze.

To serve: Allow to thaw at room temperature for 6 hours and reheat gently. Or reheat very gently while still frozen, stirring from time to time. See photograph on front cover.

Beef and mushroom cream ragoût

Pre-cooking time $2\frac{1}{2}$ hours

You will need for 4–6 servings:

2 lb. stewing steak	$\frac{1}{2}$ teaspoon salt
1 oz. butter	$\frac{1}{4}$ teaspoon pepper
1 onion, chopped	4 oz. button mushrooms,
1 oz. cornflour	sliced
1 pint cider	

To serve:
$\frac{1}{4}$ pint single cream

Cut meat into 1-inch cubes. Melt butter in a large pan and gently fry onion and meat without browning. Blend cornflour with 4 tablespoons cider in a bowl. Heat remaining cider and when boiling, pour over cornflour, stirring well. Pour liquid into pan with meat and bring to the boil, stirring all the time. Season with salt and pepper and add mushrooms. Simmer for $2\frac{1}{2}$ hours, stirring occasionally.

To freeze: Cool quickly. Turn into plastic or other suitable container, leaving $\frac{1}{2}$-inch headspace. Seal and freeze.

To serve: Allow to thaw at room temperature for 8 hours. Reheat gently and stir in $\frac{1}{4}$ pint single cream just before serving. Do not allow to boil after cream has been added.

Special turkey pie

Pre-cooking time   10 minutes
Cooking time and oven temperature, when serving
1 hour at 400°F., Gas Mark 6

You will need for 4 servings:

2 oz. mushrooms, sliced	8 oz. cooked turkey,
$1\frac{1}{2}$ oz. butter	chopped
1 oz. flour	8 oz. short crust pastry
$\frac{1}{4}$ pint cider	(see page 50) or
$\frac{1}{4}$ pint milk	1 packet frozen short
$\frac{1}{4}$ teaspoon mixed herbs	crust pastry (13 oz. size)
salt and pepper	

Lightly fry mushrooms in butter. Add flour and cook for 1 minute. Slowly blend in cider and milk. Bring to the boil, stirring all the time as the sauce thickens. Add herbs, seasoning and turkey. Allow to cool.

To freeze: Divide pastry in half and roll each half into a circle. Line an 8-inch foil pie dish with one circle and pile filling into the centre. Moisten edges with water and cover with second circle. Trim edges and decorate with pastry leaves. Freeze uncovered. When frozen, cover with double thickness foil or place in a polythene bag.

To serve: Brush with milk and place while still frozen in a moderately hot oven for 1 hour, or until pastry is golden and filling heated through.

Pizza

Pre-cooking time and oven temperature
20–25 minutes at 450°F., Gas Mark 8
Cooking time and oven temperature, when serving
45 minutes at 400°F., Gas Mark 6

You will need for 4 servings:

8 oz. plain flour	generous $\frac{1}{4}$ pint water
1 teaspoon salt	1 tablespoon oil
$\frac{1}{2}$ oz. fresh yeast, or	oil for brushing
2 teaspoons dried yeast	
and 1 teaspoon sugar	

Filling:

12 oz. tomatoes	2 oz. olives
1 large onion, chopped	1 tablespoon chopped
1 clove garlic, pressed or	parsley
finely chopped	$\frac{1}{2}$ teaspoon mixed dried
1 tablespoon oil	herbs
1 can anchovies	$\frac{1}{2}$–1 teaspoon sugar
(2 oz. size)	salt and pepper

To serve:
3 oz. grated Cheddar or
Gruyère cheese

Sieve together flour and salt. If using fresh yeast blend with water. If using dried yeast, heat water to 110°F., dissolve sugar in it and sprinkle over dried yeast. Leave for about 10 minutes or until frothy. Add to sieved flour with oil. Work to a firm dough, adding more flour if necessary until the mixture leaves the sides of the bowl clean. Place dough on a floured board and knead for about 5 minutes until it feels firm and elastic. Place in an oiled polythene bag and leave to rise until double its original size, about 1 hour at room temperature or overnight in the refrigerator. Turn dough on to board and knead for a few minutes to knock out the air bubbles. Roll out dough to a 12-inch circle and place on a greased baking tray. Turn $\frac{1}{2}$-inch of the edge over to form a rim. Prick the centre lightly with a fork. Put into a greased polythene bag and leave to rise for about 20 minutes. Brush well with oil and bake

continued on page 34

Rabbit in cider (see page 38)

Right: *Leek and lamb casserole (see page 39)*

French rabbit stew (see page 38)

continued from page 31

for 20–25 minutes in a hot oven. Remove from baking tray and cool.

Skin and chop tomatoes. Fry onion and garlic in oil until golden. Add tomatoes, chopped anchovies, leaving 6 for decoration, chopped olives, leaving 7 whole for decoration, parsley, herbs, sugar and seasoning. Bring to the boil and simmer very gently for 15 minutes. Cool. Turn mixture on to bread dough, top with reserved anchovies in a radial pattern and arrange olives in between and in the centre.

To freeze: Wrap in double thickness foil, or moisture-vapour-proof paper, or place in a polythene bag. Seal and freeze.

To serve: Sprinkle over 3 oz. grated Cheddar or Gruyère cheese and bake while still frozen for 45 minutes in a moderately hot oven.

Paella

Pre-cooking time   30 minutes
Cooking time and oven temperature, when serving
20 minutes at 350°F., Gas Mark 4

You will need for 4 servings:

2 oz. luxury margarine	1 good pinch saffron
1 tablespoon oil	powder
4 chicken drumsticks	1 can red peppers (6 oz.
or joints (boned)	size), cut into strips
1 large onion, finely	1 packet frozen peas
chopped	(4 oz. size)
2 cloves garlic, very finely	6 stuffed olives, halved
chopped or pressed	4 oz. fresh, peeled prawns
2 sticks celery	salt and freshly milled
8 oz. long grain rice	black pepper
1 pint chicken stock	¼ teaspoon oregano

Melt margarine, add oil; fry chicken until golden. Add onion, garlic and celery and cook until soft without browning. Add rice and cook for 1 minute, then add chicken stock and saffron powder. Simmer very gently for about 15 minutes or until rice had absorbed the stock. Stir in remaining ingredients and heat for about 5 minutes.

To freeze: Cool quickly. Pack into a polythene bag. Seal and freeze.

To serve: Allow to thaw at room temperature for 8 hours. Reheat in a moderate oven for 20 minutes. See photograph on page 4.

Shepherd's pie

Pre-cooking time   25 minutes
Cooking time and oven temperature, when serving
1 hour at 375°F., Gas Mark 5

You will need for 4–6 servings:

1½ lb. potatoes	1 large onion, chopped
6 tablespoons milk	1½ lb. minced beef
1 oz. butter	1 oz. flour
salt and pepper	½ pint water
1 oz. dripping	1 beef stock cube

Cook potatoes in boiling, salted water for 20 minutes or until soft. Strain and mash with milk and butter. Season to taste. Meanwhile, melt dripping in pan, add onion and fry for 5 minutes, add meat and continue frying for further 5 minutes or until meat is browned. Stir in flour and cook for 1 minute. Gradually stir in water. Crumble in stock cube and bring to the boil, stirring. Season to taste, cover and simmer for 10 minutes.

To freeze: Turn meat into a 3½-pint casserole. Top with potato, spreading right to the edge. Decorate top using a fork or round-bladed knife. Cover with double thickness foil or moisture-vapour-proof paper. Seal and freeze.

To serve: Remove foil or paper. Bake while still frozen in a moderately hot oven for 1 hour.

Rissoles

Pre-cooking time   25 minutes
Cooking time, when serving
8 minutes

You will need for 4 servings:

1 oz. lard or dripping	1 teaspoon chopped
1 oz. flour	parsley
generous ¼ pint water	pinch nutmeg
1 beef stock cube	salt and pepper
12 oz. freshly cooked,	2 eggs
minced meat	browned breadcrumbs

Melt lard or dripping in a pan, add flour and cook over a gentle heat, stirring from time to time, until brown. Remove from heat and gradually add water. Crumble in stock cube. Return to heat and bring to the boil, stirring all the time until mixture thickens. Remove from heat and cool. Add meat, parsley, nutmeg and seasoning, bind with 1 egg yolk. Lay on a flat, greased plate, covered with greaseproof paper until cold. Divide into 8 portions and form into flat cakes or cork-shaped croquettes. Beat remaining egg and egg white together. Dip meat cakes first in beaten egg and then in browned crumbs.

To freeze: Pack into a plastic container or wrap

in double thickness foil. Seal and freeze.

To serve: Allow to thaw at room temperature for 4 hours. Deep fry in fat or oil, at a temperature in which a day-old cube of bread turns brown in 1 minute, for about 8 minutes.

Chicken Simla

Pre-cooking time   1 hour

You will need for 4 servings:

4 chicken breasts	1 pint chicken stock
2 oz. butter	thinly peeled rind and
6 shallots or small onions,	juice 1 lemon
finely chopped	1 tablespoon mango
1½ oz. flour	chutney juice
1 level tablespoon	salt and pepper
curry powder	

To serve:
¼ pint single cream

Fry chicken breasts in butter on all sides until golden. Remove from pan. Add shallots and cook for about 5 minutes. Stir in flour and curry powder and cook for 2–3 minutes. Remove from heat and gradually stir in stock. Return to heat and bring to the boil, stirring all the time until mixture bubbles and thickens. Return chicken to pan with lemon rind and juice and chutney juice. Season to taste and simmer for 45 minutes. Remove lemon rind.

To freeze: Cool quickly. Turn into plastic or other suitable container. Seal and freeze.

To serve: Allow to thaw at room temperature for 6 hours. Reheat gently in a saucepan. Stir in

Lamb curry

¼ pint single cream just before serving. Do not allow to boil after cream has been added. Serve with rice and fried almonds.

Lamb curry

Pre-cooking time   1½ hours

You will need for 4 servings:

1 lb. shoulder of lamb,	½ teaspoon chilli powder
cut in 1-inch cubes	½ teaspoon curry powder
1 carton natural yoghourt	¼ teaspoon mixed spice
4 cloves	2–3 cardamoms (optional)
4 black peppercorns	1 can tomatoes (8 oz. size)
two ½-inch sticks cinnamon	½ pint water
1 teaspoon turmeric	2 potatoes, peeled and
4 large onions,	diced (optional)
finely sliced	salt
4 oz. butter	
½ teaspoon paprika pepper	

Put the meat in a mixing bowl with the yoghourt, 2 cloves, 2 peppercorns, 1 stick of cinnamon and half the turmeric. Mix well and leave for at least 1 hour. Fry the onions in the butter until golden brown. Add the remaining spices and fry for a few minutes. Add the meat, together with the marinade and cook, stirring, over a moderate heat for 5 minutes. Add the tomatoes, water and potatoes, if used, and stir well. Cover and simmer for 1–1¼ hours, until the lamb is tender. Adjust seasoning. See photograph below.

To freeze: Cool quickly. Turn into a plastic or other suitable container. Seal and freeze.

To serve: Allow to thaw at room temperature for 6 hours. Reheat gently and serve on a bed of boiled or fried rice.

Beef curry

Pre-cooking time   2¾ hours

You will need for 6 servings:

1½ lb. chuck beef	2 beef stock cubes
1½ oz. flour	1 small cooking apple,
1 level tablespoon curry	peeled and chopped
powder	2 tablespoons chutney
salt and pepper	2 tablespoons honey
3 tablespoons oil	grated rind and juice
2 large onions, chopped	1 lemon
1½ pints water	

To serve:
bay leaves to garnish

Cut meat into 1-inch cubes and toss in flour, seasoned with curry powder and salt and pepper. Heat oil in pan, add onions and fry for about 5 minutes. Add meat, with any remaining flour, and brown. Remove from heat and gradually stir in water. Return to heat and bring to boil, stirring all the time until mixture bubbles and thickens. Crumble in stock cubes. Add cooking apple, chutney, honey and lemon rind and juice. Cover and simmer gently for 2½ hours. Taste and adjust seasoning.
To freeze: Cool quickly. Pour into plastic or other suitable container, leaving ½-inch headspace. Seal and freeze.
To serve: Either allow to thaw at room temperature for 6–8 hours and reheat gently or reheat very gently in a saucepan when still frozen. Serve with rice, and garnish with bay leaves.

Loosening Herby beef loaf in tin

Pork chops with pears and apricots

Pre-cooking time   25 minutes

You will need for 4 servings:

4 oz. dried whole apricots	¼ teaspoon ground ginger
4 pork chops	salt and pepper
1 tablespoon oil	2 oz. seedless raisins
1 tablespoon flour	1 large ripe pear
1 bottle dry ginger ale	
(8 fl. oz. size)	**To serve:**
	parsley for garnish

Soak the apricots in cold water overnight. Fry the chops in the oil for about 15 minutes, turning once. Remove from the pan and place in a plastic or other suitable container. Pour off any excess fat from pan, stir in the flour and cook for a minute. Stir in the dry ginger and ¼ pint juice from the apricots. Bring to the boil, stirring all the time until mixture bubbles and thickens, season with ginger and salt and pepper. Add the raisins and simmer gently for 5 minutes. Peel and core the pear, slice and add to the sauce with the drained apricots.
To freeze: Pour the sauce over the chops. Cool quickly, seal and freeze.
To serve: Allow to thaw at room temperature for 6 hours. Reheat gently in a saucepan. Arrange pork chops in serving dish with the fruit, pour over a little of the sauce and garnish with sprigs of parsley. Serve the remaining sauce separately. See colour photograph on page 21.

Making a good centre overlap

Jugged hare

Pre-cooking time   2½–3 hours

You will need for 6 servings:

1 hare	1½ pints stock
1 oz. flour	grated rind and juice
salt and pepper	1 lemon
6 oz. fat bacon,	1 bouquet garni
cut in one piece	¼ pint port wine
2 large onions	blood of the hare
8 cloves	1 tablespoon redcurrant
3 carrots, chopped	jelly
1 stick celery, chopped	

Joint hare and toss in flour, seasoned with salt and pepper. Cut bacon in 1-inch cubes and fry over low heat until fat runs. Insert 4 cloves into each onion. Add hare and vegetables and fry for about 10 minutes. Add stock, lemon rind and juice and bouquet garni. Bring to boil and simmer very gently for 2–2½ hours, depending on the size and age of the hare. Mix ¼ pint of the hot stock with the blood of the hare and port. Pour into saucepan with redcurrant jelly and stir over heat until thickened. Season.
To freeze: Place joints in plastic or other suitable container. Strain over sauce leaving ½-inch headspace. Cool quickly, seal and freeze.
To serve: Allow to thaw at room temperature for 6–8 hours. Reheat gently, taking care that the sauce does not curdle. Serve with forcemeat balls (see above, right).

Final wrapping before placing in freezer

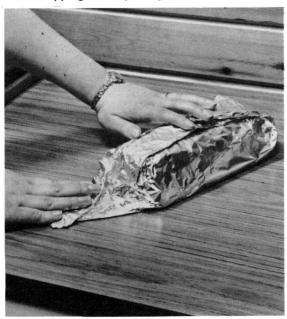

Forcemeat balls

Pre-cooking time   5 minutes
Cooking time, when serving
3–5 minutes

You will need for 6 servings:

1 small onion, finely	2 teaspoons chopped
chopped	parsley
1 rasher streaky bacon,	pinch dried marjoram
finely chopped	salt and pepper
2 oz. fresh white	2 eggs, beaten
breadcrumbs	browned breadcrumbs
½ oz. shredded suet	

Fry onion with bacon until onion is soft. Add breadcrumbs, suet, parsley, marjoram and salt and pepper. Bind with enough beaten egg to form a fairly stiff consistency. Roll into balls the size of a walnut. Dip in remaining beaten egg and then in browned breadcrumbs.
To freeze: Wrap in double thickness foil or place in a polythene bag. Seal and freeze.
To serve: Allow to thaw at room temperature for 3 hours. Fry in deep fat for about 5 minutes until golden brown. Serve with jugged hare.

Herby beef loaf

Pre-cooking time and oven temperature
1¼ hours at 350°F., Gas Mark 4
Cooking time and oven temperature, when serving
20–25 minutes at 325°F., Gas Mark 3 or
55 minutes at 350°F., Gas Mark 4

You will need for 4 servings:

2 oz. butter	½ teaspoon ground nutmeg
1 oz. browned breadcrumbs	2 oz. fresh white
8 oz. lean minced beef	breadcrumbs
1 onion, finely chopped	1 egg, beaten
¾ teaspoon dried mixed	¼ pint stock
herbs	salt and freshly milled
	black pepper

Well butter a 5 inch cake tin or 1 lb. loaf tin. Coat inside of tin with browned crumbs. Melt remaining butter in pan and fry beef and onion for about 10 minutes. Add remaining ingredients and turn into prepared tin. Cover with foil and bake in a moderate oven for 1 hour.
To freeze: Cool quickly, then turn out of tin, wrap in foil and freeze. See photographs on the left.
To serve: Either allow to thaw at room temperature for 8 hours and reheat in the tin in oven for 20–25 minutes or place frozen in a moderate oven for 55 minutes, or until heated through. Turn out of tin and serve.

Rabbit in cider

Pre-cooking time   1 hour

You will need for 4 servings:

1 rabbit, jointed	¼ pint water
1 oz. flour	½ pint dry cider
salt and pepper	1 bay leaf
1½ oz. butter	grated rind ½ lemon
1 large onion, chopped	1 tablespoon sultanas
4 oz. piece bacon, diced	

To serve:

parsley sprigs to garnish	large croûtons

Toss the rabbit joints in the flour, seasoned with salt and pepper. Melt the butter in a saucepan and fry the joints slowly until golden all over; remove from the pan. Fry the onion and bacon, sprinkle in any remaining flour, stir and cook for 1 minute. Remove from the heat and stir in the water and cider. Return to the heat and bring to the boil, stirring all the time until sauce bubbles and thickens. Add the bay leaf, lemon rind and sultanas and replace the rabbit. Cover and simmer gently for about 1 hour or until rabbit is tender. Adjust seasoning.
To freeze: Cool quickly. Turn into a plastic or other suitable container. Seal and freeze.
To serve: Allow to thaw at room temperature for 6 hours. Reheat gently and serve garnished with parsley sprigs and large croûtons. See colour photograph on page 32.

French rabbit stew

Pre-cooking time and oven temperature
2 hours at 325°F., Gas Mark 3

You will need for 4 servings:

1½ lb. rabbit pieces	8 oz. prunes, stoned
1 oz. lard	1 bouquet garni
2–3 onions, sliced	1 oz. flour
1 lb. carrots, peeled and sliced	1 pint chicken stock
	salt and pepper

Fry rabbit in hot lard until evenly browned. Place in casserole with onions, carrots, prunes and bouquet garni. Add flour to fat in pan and cook until brown. Remove from heat and gradually add stock. Return to heat and bring to boil, stirring all the time until mixture bubbles and thickens. Season to taste and pour into casserole. Cover and place in a moderate oven for 1½ hours. Remove bouquet garni. See colour photograph on page 32.
To freeze: Cool quickly. Turn into plastic or other suitable container, leaving ½-inch head-space.
To serve: Allow to thaw at room temperature for 8 hours. Reheat gently in a saucepan.

Devilled kidneys

Pre-cooking time   20 minutes

You will need for 4 servings:

4 pig's kidneys	½ pint water
1 oz. flour	1 beef stock cube
salt and pepper	1 tablespoon made mustard
2 oz. butter	½ teaspoon Worcestershire sauce
1 medium sized onion, chopped	

Skin, core and slice kidneys and toss in flour, seasoned with salt and pepper. Melt butter in pan and gently fry onion for about 5 minutes or until soft. Add kidneys and any remaining flour and fry for 10 minutes. Stir in water and bring slowly to the boil. Crumble in stock cube, add mustard and Worcestershire sauce and continue cooking for 5 minutes. Season to taste.
To freeze: Cool quickly. Pack into plastic or other suitable container, leaving ½-inch head-space. Seal and freeze.
To serve: Turn into saucepan and reheat gently or allow to thaw at room temperature for 8 hours, then reheat.

Spare ribs of pork with barbecue sauce

Pre-cooking time   25 minutes

You will need for 4 servings:

½ oz. dripping	2 tablespoons soft brown sugar
4 spare rib pork chops, about 2 lb.	3 tablespoons vinegar
1 large onion, finely chopped	1 teaspoon Worcestershire sauce
pinch garlic powder	½ teaspoon salt
1 can tomato purée (2¼ oz. size)	pinch cayenne pepper
4 tablespoons water	2 teaspoons dry mustard
	pinch mixed herbs

Melt dripping in a shallow pan and quickly brown meat on both sides, lift out on to a plate. Lightly fry onion for 5 minutes, adding remaining ingredients, stir and bring to the boil. Return meat to the pan. Cover and simmer gently for 15 minutes.
To freeze: Cool quickly. Pack into a large polythene bag, seal and freeze.
To serve: Allow to thaw at room temperature for 8 hours. Reheat gently.

Quiche Lorraine

Quiche Lorraine

Pre-cooking time and oven temperature
15 minutes at 400 °F., Gas Mark 6
then 25 minutes at 350 °F., Gas Mark 4
Cooking time and oven temperature, when serving
15 minutes at 350 °F., Gas Mark 4

You will need for 4 servings:

6 oz. short crust pastry (see page 50) or 1 packet frozen short crust pastry ($7\frac{1}{2}$ oz. size)	generous $\frac{1}{4}$ pint milk 2 eggs, beaten salt and pepper 1 oz. Cheddar cheese, grated
4 oz. streaky bacon, chopped	
1 medium sized onion, chopped	

To serve:
watercress to garnish

Roll out pastry and use to line a 7-inch flan ring. Prick base and chill. Fill centre with greaseproof paper or foil and baking beans and bake in a moderately hot oven for 10 minutes. Remove greaseproof paper or foil and beans and bake for a further 5 minutes. Meanwhile, fry bacon over a gentle heat with onion, until onion is soft. Place in bottom of flan case. Add milk to eggs and season. Pour into flan case. Sprinkle with cheese and bake in a moderate oven for 25 minutes or until set.

To freeze: Cool quickly. Wrap in double thickness foil or place in a polythene bag and seal. Freeze.

To serve: Thaw in refrigerator for 24 hours if serving cold. Allow to thaw at room temperature for 6 hours and reheat in a moderate oven for 15 minutes if serving hot and garnish with watercress. See photograph above.

Leek and lamb casserole

Pre-cooking time and oven temperature
$2\frac{1}{4}$ hours at 325 °F., Gas Mark 3

You will need for 4 servings:

$1\frac{1}{2}$ lb. middle or best end neck of lamb	1 oz. dripping 1 can tomatoes (8 oz. size)
2 oz. flour	1 pint water
1 teaspoon salt	1 tablespoon tomato purée
$\frac{1}{4}$ teaspoon pepper	$\frac{1}{2}$ teaspoon dried thyme
3 leeks	

Toss lamb in flour seasoned with salt and pepper. Coarsely slice leeks. Melt dripping in large pan and fry lamb on all sides to brown. Place in a casserole. Fry leeks gently for 2 minutes and place in casserole with drained tomatoes, reserving juice. Add remaining flour to fat in pan, cook for 1 minute. Stir in water, juice from canned tomatoes, tomato purée and thyme. Bring to the boil, stirring. Pour over lamb. Cover and bake in a moderate oven for 2 hours.

To freeze: Cool quickly. Pack into plastic or other suitable container. Seal and freeze.

To serve: Allow to thaw at room temperature for 6–8 hours. Reheat gently in a saucepan. See colour photograph on page 33.

Veal chops in wine

Pre-cooking time and oven temperature
40 minutes at 350°F., Gas Mark 4

You will need for 4 servings:

4 veal chops	½ pint chicken stock
1 oz. flour	1 can tomato purée
salt and pepper	(2¼ oz. size)
2 oz. butter	1 bouquet garni
¼ pint white wine	

Dust chops with flour, seasoned with salt and pepper. Melt butter in pan and fry chops on both sides until brown. Place in a casserole. Add remaining flour to fat in pan and cook for 1 minute. Remove from heat and gradually stir in wine, stock and tomato purée. Return to heat and bring to boil, stirring all the time until mixture bubbles and thickens. Add bouquet garni and season to taste. Pour over chops and bake in a moderate oven for 30 minutes. Remove bouquet garni.

To freeze: Cool quickly. Turn into plastic or other suitable container. Seal and freeze.

To serve: Allow to thaw at room temperature for 8 hours. Reheat gently in a saucepan.

Lamb cutlets in pastry

Pre-cooking time   10 minutes
Cooking time and oven temperature, when serving
40 minutes at 425°F., Gas Mark 7

You will need for 4 servings:

4 neck cutlets of lamb	4 oz. puff pastry (see page
1 oz. butter	51) or 7½ oz. packet
salt and pepper	frozen puff pastry

To serve:

little beaten egg	parsley to garnish

Trim the meat from the bone 1½ inches from the top of each cutlet. Put in a grill pan, dot with butter and season with salt and pepper. Grill for about 10 minutes, or until tender, turning once. Cool. Roll out the pastry and cut into four squares. Brush the edges with water. Place a cutlet in the centre of each square of pastry and wrap round, placing the sealed edges underneath and leaving the bone at the top free. Roll out the trimmings and cut into leaves. Brush with water and place two leaves on top of each cutlet.

To freeze: Freeze uncovered. When frozen, wrap in double thickness foil or moisture-vapour-proof paper and seal.

To serve: Brush pastry well with beaten egg. Place in a hot oven for about 40 minutes or until pastry is golden brown. Place cutlet frills on the bones. Serve with peas and broccoli and garnish with parsley. See photograph on back cover.

Cornish pasties

Cooking time and oven temperature, when serving
10 minutes at 400°F., Gas Mark 6 then
1 hour at 350°F., Gas Mark 4

You will need for 4 servings:

12 oz. lean braising steak	3 tablespoons stock or
2 medium sized potatoes,	water
peeled and cut into	8 oz. short crust pastry
¼-inch pieces	(see page 50) or
1 large onion, chopped	1 packet frozen short
salt and pepper	crust pastry (13 oz. size)

Cut steak into ¼-inch cubes, and put into a basin with potatoes and onion. Season with salt and pepper. Mix well and moisten with stock or water. Roll out pastry and cut into four 6-inch circles. Divide filling among the circles, placing it in the centre. Damp edges of pastry and bring to centre. Seal edges and flute.

To freeze: Wrap in moisture-vapour-proof paper or double thickness foil, or put in a polythene bag. Seal and freeze.

To serve: Place on a baking sheet and bake in a moderately hot oven for 10 minutes, then lower heat to moderate and cook for a further 1 hour. If pastry becomes too brown during cooking, cover with foil.

Liver casserole

Pre-cooking time and oven temperature
2 hours at 350°F., Gas Mark 4

You will need for 4 servings:

1 lb. ox liver, cut in	1 stick celery, chopped
thin slices	2 onions, chopped
1 oz. flour	1 pint water
salt and pepper	1 beef stock cube
2 oz. lard	1 teaspoon mixed herbs
1 lb. carrots, peeled	
and chopped	

Toss liver in flour, seasoned with salt and pepper. Melt lard in pan and fry liver on both sides to seal. Place in a casserole. Lightly fry carrots, celery and onion for 5 minutes. Add to meat. Add any remaining flour to fat in pan and allow to brown. Remove from heat and gradually add water. Crumble in stock cube, add herbs and bring to the boil, stirring all the time until mixture bubbles and thickens. Season to taste and pour over liver and vegetables. Cover and place in a moderate oven for $1\frac{1}{2}$ hours.

To freeze: Cool quickly. Turn into plastic or other suitable container, leaving $\frac{1}{2}$-inch headspace. Seal and freeze.

To serve: Allow to thaw at room temperature for 8 hours. Reheat gently in a saucepan.

Stuffed peppers

Pre-cooking time   25 minutes
Cooking time and oven temperature, when serving
30–40 minutes at 375°F., Gas Mark 5

You will need for 4 servings:

4 green peppers	3 large carrots, peeled
salt and pepper	and chopped
2 teaspoons oil	2 cloves garlic
2 medium sized onions,	12 oz. raw minced beef
chopped	

To serve:
cheese sauce (see page 17)

Cut tops off peppers and scoop out seeds. Boil peppers in salted water with "lids" for 5 minutes. Drain. Heat oil in pan and fry onions, carrots, garlic and beef slowly for 20 minutes. Season well. Divide mixture among pepper cases. Top with "lids".

To freeze: Wrap each pepper separately in double thickness foil and freeze.

To serve: Allow to thaw at room temperature for 6 hours. Bake in a moderately hot oven for 30–40 minutes or until peppers are tender. Serve with cheese sauce.

Potato topped fish pie

Pre-cooking time   30 minutes
Cooking time and oven temperature, when serving
1 hour at 375°F., Gas Mark 5

You will need for 4 servings:

1 lb. smoked haddock	2 oz. butter
fillet	1 oz. flour
1 pint milk	salt and pepper
1 bay leaf	1 tablespoon chopped
1 onion	parsley
6 peppercorns	$1\frac{1}{2}$ lb. potatoes

Put haddock with all the milk, less 6 tablespoons, bay leaf, onion and peppercorns, in saucepan. Cover and poach gently for about 10 minutes or until fish flakes easily. Remove from heat, remove fish and flake, discarding skin. Strain milk. Melt 1 oz. butter in pan, add flour and cook for 1 minute. Remove from heat and gradually stir in strained milk from fish. Return to heat and bring to the boil, stirring all the time until mixture bubbles and thickens. Add fish and parsley and season to taste. Meanwhile cook peeled potatoes in boiling, salted water for 20 minutes or until soft. Strain and mash with remaining 6 tablespoons milk and 1 oz. butter. Season to taste.

To freeze: Pour fish mixture into 3 pint foil dish or other suitable container. Top with potato and decorate top using a fork or round-bladed knife. Cover with double thickness foil and freeze.

To serve: Remove foil or paper. Brush with milk and bake while still frozen in a moderately hot oven for 1 hour.

Breton scallops

Pre-cooking time   20 minutes
Cooking time and oven temperature, when serving
15 minutes at 375°F., Gas Mark 5

You will need for 4 servings:

8 scallops	$\frac{1}{2}$ oz. flour
1 small onion	$\frac{1}{4}$ pint milk
$\frac{1}{2}$ pint white wine	salt and pepper
1 oz. butter	

To serve:

$\frac{1}{8}$ pint double cream	1 tablespoon grated
	Parmesan cheese

Wash scallops thoroughly. Put scallops, onion and wine into a saucepan. Simmer until scallops become opaque, about 5 to 7 minutes. Remove scallops and onion with a draining spoon and chop. Reduce wine to $\frac{1}{8}$ pint. Melt butter in a pan, stir in flour and cook for 1 minute. Remove from heat and gradually stir in milk. Return to heat, bring to the boil, stirring all the time until thickened. Add wine, scallops and onion. Season to taste.

To freeze: Cool quickly. Turn into plastic or other suitable container, leaving $\frac{1}{2}$-inch headspace. Seal and freeze.

To serve: Allow to thaw at room temperature for 5 hours. Divide among 4 ramekin dishes. Whip $\frac{1}{8}$ pint double cream and stir in 1 tablespoon grated Parmesan cheese. Spoon over scallops. Bake in a moderately hot oven for 15 minutes or until scallops are heated through and top is golden, or put under a hot grill.

Salmon mousse

Pre-cooking time   10 minutes

You will need for 4–6 servings:

2 eggs, separated
½ pint freshly made
  Béchamel sauce
  (see page 15)
1 can salmon (7½ oz. size)

2 tablespoons tomato purée
¼ pint aspic jelly, made up
  to treble strength
salt and pepper

To serve:
cucumber slices

watercress sprig

Beat yolks into hot sauce. Flake salmon and add, with juice from can and tomato purée. Carefully stir in aspic jelly. Season to taste with salt and pepper. Whisk egg whites until stiff and peaky and fold into mixture. Turn into a 1½ pint mould, foil dish or 6-inch cake tin and leave to set.
To freeze: When set, cover with double thickness foil, or moisture-vapour-proof paper. Seal and freeze.
To serve: Allow to thaw in the refrigerator for 24 hours. Turn out and garnish with halved cucumber slices and watercress. See photograph above.

Salmon mousse

Fishcakes

Cooking time when serving 8 minutes

You will need for 4 servings:

8 oz. freshly cooked
  fish, flaked
8 oz. freshly cooked
  mashed potato
½ oz. butter
1 small tin anchovies,
  drained and chopped

2 teaspoons chopped
  parsley
2 eggs
salt and pepper
browned breadcrumbs

Mix fish with potatoes, butter, anchovies and parsley. Beat 1 egg, add to fish mixture, and season with salt and pepper. Form into 8 flat cakes. Beat other egg, dip cakes in this, then in breadcrumbs.
To freeze: Pack into a plastic container or wrap in double thickness foil. Seal and freeze.
To serve: Allow to thaw at room temperature for 4 hours. Deep fry in hot fat or oil for about 8 minutes.

cakes, bread and pastry

All sorts of teatime delights—cakes, bread and pastry—can be satisfactorily stored in the freezer, and be produced as required.

Bread making is perhaps not for all of us, but bought bread can be successfully stored in the freezer for limited periods. Packs of sandwiches freeze particularly well. An hour's work once a month will give you sufficient packs of assorted sandwiches for the average family's needs. Once you have experienced the wonderful relief of being able to tell your family to "help themselves from the freezer", when sandwiches are needed, you will never go back to the old panic routine of hastily buttering bread and opening cans.

Most housewives take a pride in their home-baked cakes, but the time taken to prepare a mixture for three or four cakes is just about the same as for one. So why not make a batch, then store in your freezer? Cakes from the freezer taste as fresh as if baked the day before and even icings and decorations are not a problem. If there is a run on home-baked cakes, you may need to bake again after three weeks, but if for some reason not many cakes are eaten, the ones you have in store will keep well for several weeks longer and you can postpone the usual cake-making session.

Scones

Pre-cooking time and oven temperature
10 minutes at 425°F., Gas Mark 7

You will need for 24 scones:

1 lb. plain flour	4 teaspoons cream of
1 teaspoon salt	tartar
2 teaspoons bicarbonate	3 oz. butter
of soda	$\frac{1}{2}$ pint milk

Sieve together flour, salt, bicarbonate of soda and cream of tartar. Rub in butter until mixture resembles fine breadcrumbs. Add milk and bind together to form a soft dough. Roll out on a floured board to $\frac{1}{2}$-inch thickness. Cut out rounds with a 2-inch cutter. Place on greased baking trays and bake in a hot oven for about 10 minutes or until well risen and brown. Remove from trays and cool on a rack.

To freeze: Pack into a plastic container or wrap in double thickness foil. Seal and freeze.

To serve: Allow to thaw at room temperature for about $1\frac{1}{2}$–2 hours. Serve with butter and jam.

Note: If preferred, use self-raising flour and omit bicarbonate of soda and cream of tartar.

Variations:

Fruit scones: Add 4 oz. mixed currants and sultanas and 2 oz. castor sugar after rubbing in the butter.

Cheese scones: Sieve $\frac{1}{4}$ teaspoon cayenne pepper with flour and other ingredients. Add 6 oz. grated strong Cheddar cheese after rubbing in the butter.

Family fruit cake

Pre-cooking time and oven temperature
1–$1\frac{1}{4}$ hours at 350°F., Gas Mark 4

You will need:

4 oz. butter	3 oz. currants
4 oz. castor sugar	3 oz. sultanas
2 eggs, beaten	2 oz. raisins
8 oz. self-raising flour	2–3 tablespoons milk

Beat butter and sugar together until light and fluffy. Gradually beat in eggs, adding a tablespoon of sieved flour with the last amount of egg. Fold in sieved flour and cleaned fruit alternately. Add milk to give a soft dropping consistency. Turn into a greased and lined 6-inch cake tin and

Cherry and walnut cake (see right)

Apricot cheesecake (see page 62)

bake in a moderate oven for $1-1\frac{1}{4}$ hours. Turn out of the tin and cool on a rack.

To freeze: Wrap in moisture-vapour-proof paper or double thickness foil. Seal and freeze.

To serve: Allow to thaw at room temperature for 4 hours.

Rich chocolate cake

Pre-cooking time and oven temperature
50 minutes at 350°F., Gas Mark 4

You will need:

8 oz. butter	4 eggs, beaten
6 oz. soft brown sugar	6 oz. self-raising flour
6 oz. black treacle	2 oz. cocoa

Butter icing:

1 oz. butter	$1\frac{1}{2}$ oz. plain chocolate
2 oz. icing sugar	1 teaspoon water

Cream together butter, sugar and treacle. Gradually beat in eggs, adding a tablespoon of sieved flour with the last amount of egg. Sieve together flour and cocoa and fold into creamed mixture. Turn into two greased and lined 8- or 9-inch sandwich tins. Bake in a moderate oven for about 50 minutes. Turn out and cool.

Cream butter for icing and beat in sieved icing sugar until light and fluffy. Melt chocolate with water in basin over hot water. Beat into butter and sugar. Sandwich cakes together with icing.

To freeze: Wrap in moisture-vapour-proof paper or foil or place in a polythene bag. Seal and freeze.

To serve: Allow to thaw at room temperature for 4 hours.

Cherry and walnut cake

Pre-cooking time and oven temperature
about $1-1\frac{1}{4}$ hours at 350°., Gas Mark 4

You will need:

3 oz. glacé cherries, quartered	3 eggs, beaten
	8 oz. self-raising flour
6 oz. butter	1 oz. walnut halves,
6 oz. castor sugar	roughly chopped

Wash cherries in warm water and dry thoroughly with kitchen paper. Cream butter and sugar until light and fluffy. Gradually beat in eggs, adding a tablespoon of the sieved flour with the last amount of egg. Fold in sieved flour, walnuts and cherries. Turn into a greased and lined 7-inch round cake tin. Bake in a moderate oven for $1-1\frac{1}{4}$ hours, or until cake springs back when lightly touched with the tip of the finger. Turn out and cool.

To freeze: Wrap in moisture-vapour-proof paper or double thickness foil. Seal and freeze.

To serve: Allow to thaw at room temperature for 4 hours. See colour photograph on left.

Whisked sponge flan

Pre-cooking time and oven temperature
about 20 minutes at 375°F., Gas Mark 5

You will need for an 8-inch flan:

2 eggs	2 oz. self-raising flour
2 oz. castor sugar	

Whisk eggs and sugar together until thick and creamy and whisk leaves a trail when lifted out of the mixture. Carefully fold in sieved flour and turn into a well greased 8-inch sponge flan tin. Bake in a moderately hot oven for about 20 minutes or until sponge springs back when lightly touched with the tip of the finger. Turn out and cool.

Note: If you have more than one sponge flan tin, it is obviously more practical to make up more than one at a time.

To freeze: Wrap in a polythene bag. Seal and freeze.

To prepare for use: Allow to thaw at room temperature for 1 hour. Use as a case for sweet flans.

Coffee gâteau

Pre-cooking time and oven temperature
15 minutes at 400°F., Gas Mark 6

You will need:

3 large eggs	4 oz. self-raising flour
3 oz. castor sugar	

Coffee icing:

6 oz. butter	3 tablespoons coffee
12 oz. icing sugar, sieved	essence

To serve:
1 packet cats' tongue biscuits

Whisk eggs and sugar till thick and creamy and whisk leaves a trail when lifted out of the mixture. Fold in sifted flour. Pour into a greased and lined 13-inch by 11-inch Swiss roll tin. Bake in a moderately hot oven for about 15 minutes, or until cake springs back when lightly touched with the tip of the finger. Turn out and cool.

Cream butter for icing, gradually beat in sieved icing sugar and coffee essence. Cut cake in 3 lengthways. Sandwich together with two layers of coffee icing. Cover sides and top of gâteau with remaining coffee icing. Make diagonal lines across the top with a fork.

To freeze: Place on a plate and freeze uncovered. When frozen, wrap in moisture-vapour-proof paper or double thickness foil and seal.

To serve: Uncover and allow to thaw at room temperature for 4 hours. Place three half cats' tongue biscuits in the centre at different angles. Press cats' tongue biscuits close together into sides. See photograph below.

Coffee whirl cake

Pre-cooking time and oven temperature
1 hour at 350°F., Gas Mark 4

You will need:

8 oz. self-raising flour	3 eggs, beaten
6 oz. butter	3 tablespoons coffee
6 oz. castor sugar	essence

Coffee icing:

4 oz. butter	2 tablespoons coffee
8 oz. icing sugar, sieved	essence

Sift flour. Cream butter and sugar until light and fluffy. Beat in eggs gradually, adding a tablespoon of the sieved flour with the last amount of egg. Fold in remaining flour. Divide mixture into two and stir coffee essence into one half. Place a tablespoon of plain and a tablespoon of coffee mixture alternately over the base of a greased and lined 8-inch cake tin until all the mixture is used. Smooth top with a palette knife. Bake in a moderate oven for 1 hour or until top springs back when lightly touched with the tip of the finger. Turn out and cool. Cream butter for icing until light, then gradually beat in icing sugar and coffee essence. Spread over the top and sides of the cake and whirl up with a knife.

To freeze: Place on a plate and freeze uncovered. When frozen, wrap in double thickness foil or moisture-vapour-proof paper and seal.

To serve: Uncover and allow to thaw at room temperature for 4 hours. See photograph on page 47.

Coffee gâteau

Chocolate clock cake

Pre-cooking time and oven temperature
about 45 minutes at 350°F., Gas Mark 4

You will need:

3 eggs	3 oz. self-raising flour
3 oz. castor sugar	2 tablespoons oil

Chocolate butter icing:

2 oz. butter	2 tablespoons drinking
2 oz. icing sugar, sieved	chocolate powder

Chocolate icing:

small can evaporated	6 oz. plain chocolate
milk	

Marzipan:

2 oz. bought marzipan	red food colouring

Whisk eggs and sugar together until thick and creamy and whisk leaves a trail when lifted out of the mixture. Fold in sieved flour, then oil. Turn into a greased and lined 7-inch cake tin. Bake in a moderate oven for about 45 minutes or until cake springs back when lightly touched with the tip of a finger. Turn out and cool.

Cream butter and gradually beat in sieved icing sugar and chocolate powder. When cake is cold, split in half and sandwich together with this.

Place cake on a rack. Heat evaporated milk in a saucepan until very hot but not boiling. Remove from heat and stir in broken-up chocolate. Mix until chocolate has dissolved, returning to a gentle heat if necessary. Cool icing, stirring all the time until it coats the back of a wooden spoon. Pour over cake spreading with a palette knife if necessary and leave to set. Colour marzipan with a few drops of red colouring. Roll out to about $\frac{1}{4}$-inch thickness and, using a stencil, cut out figures for clock face and place on cake. Cut out the two hands and place in position.

To freeze: Carefully place on a plate and freeze uncovered. When frozen, wrap very carefully in moisture-vapour-proof paper and seal.

To serve: Allow to thaw at room temperature for 6 hours.

Coffee whirl cake

Racing track cake

Pre-cooking time and oven temperature
45 minutes–1 hour at 350°F., Gas Mark 4

You will need:

12 oz. butter	6 eggs, beaten
12 oz. castor sugar	12 oz. self-raising flour

Lemon butter icing:

6 oz. butter	milk to mix
grated rind 2 lemons	sieved apricot jam
12 oz. icing sugar, sieved	

Fondant icing:

2 oz. butter	1 packet chocolate
juice 2 lemons	finger biscuits
green colouring	coffee essence
1½ lb. icing sugar, sieved	sieved apricot jam

Cream butter and sugar together until light and fluffy. Gradually beat in eggs, adding a tablespoon of sieved flour with the last amount of egg. Fold in remaining sieved flour. Divide cake mixture between a greased and lined 6-inch round cake tin and a greased and lined 6-inch square cake tin. Bake in a moderate oven for 45 minutes to 1 hour or until cakes spring back when lightly touched with the tip of the finger. Turn out and cool on a rack.
Cream butter for icing and gradually beat in lemon rind, icing sugar and enough milk to give spreading consistency. Split cakes in half, divide most of the icing between them and sandwich together again. Divide round cake in half to make two semi-circles, spread the remaining butter icing on the cut ends and place on opposite ends of the square cake to form an oval. Brush the whole of the cake with apricot jam.
Put butter and lemon juice for fondant icing into a pan and heat gently until the butter has just melted. Stir in enough green colouring to make this syrup a strong green. Add 8 oz. of the icing sugar and stir the mixture over a low heat, without letting it simmer, until all the sugar has dissolved. Then bring the mixture up to simmering point and let it simmer gently for just 2 minutes until it is just boiling. Remove the pan from the heat, stir in another 8 oz. icing sugar and beat well with a wooden spoon. Pour the mixture into a bowl and add enough of the remaining sugar, a tablespoon at a time, to make it the consistency of a soft, moulding paste. Sprinkle the working surface liberally with sieved icing sugar and knead the paste until smooth. Work in more green colouring at this stage if necessary. Roll out three-quarters of the icing with a well sugared rolling pin to a large oval. Wrap over the rolling pin, and place carefully over cake. Trim edges and press icing into sides of cake, smoothing away any creases. Cut chocolate biscuits to size, brush with apricot jam and stick to the sides of the cake to form a fence. Colour fondant icing trimmings dark brown with coffee essence and cut into thin strips. Brush with apricot jam and place on top of the cake to form a track.
To freeze: Freeze uncovered. When frozen, wrap in moisture-vapour-proof paper or double thickness foil and seal.
To serve: Allow to thaw at room temperature for 8 hours. Place racing flags, starting gates and toy racing cars on the top.

White bread

Cooking time and oven temperature
30–40 minutes at 450°F., Gas Mark 8

You will need for 1 large loaf or 2 small loaves

Dry mix:

1 lb. plain flour	½ oz. lard rubbed into flour
2 level teaspoons salt	

Yeast liquid:
Mix ½ oz. fresh yeast in ½ pint water or dissolve 1 teaspoon sugar in ½ pint warm (110°F.) water, sprinkle on 2 level teaspoons dried yeast. Leave until frothy (about 10 minutes).

Mix dry ingredients with yeast liquid using a wooden fork or spoon, then work with one hand to a firm dough adding extra flour, if needed, until dough leaves sides of the bowl clean. Turn on to a lightly floured board and knead thoroughly to stretch and develop dough. To do this, fold dough towards you, then push down and away with palm of hand. Repeat for about 10 minutes until dough feels firm and elastic and no longer sticky. After kneading shape dough into a ball. Place in a large, lightly greased polythene bag.
To freeze unrisen dough: Seal bag tightly and place in freezer.
Note: As dough might rise slightly before freezing, leave 1-inch space for expansion in the bag.
To freeze risen dough: Loosely tie bag, leaving room for dough to rise. Allow to rise until double in size:–

> Quick rise: 45–60 minutes in a warm place.
> Slower rise: 2 hours average room temperature.
> Overnight rise: up to 12 hours in a cold larder or refrigerator.

Risen dough springs back when pressed with a lightly floured finger. Turn risen dough on to a lightly floured board and flatten firmly with the knuckles to knock out air bubbles, then knead

Hot cross buns

until firm. Place in lightly greased polythene bag, tightly seal and place in freezer.

To prepare unrisen dough for use: Thaw about 5–6 hours at room temperature, then leave to rise and spring back, as above.

To prepare risen dough for use: Thaw about 5–6 hours at room temperature.

To shape the dough: For tin loaves, divide dough into the quantity required (i.e. leave whole for a large loaf, or divide into two for two small loaves) and shape the loaves as follows. Flatten dough with the knuckles to an oblong the same width as the tin. Fold in three and turn over so that seam is underneath. Smooth over the top and tuck in the ends. The loaves are now ready to rise again (this is known as proving). Put tins inside a greased polythene bag and leave until dough rises to tops of tins. This takes 30–40 minutes at room temperature, or leave in a refrigerator if a slow rising is more convenient. Remove from polythene bag and bake loaves in centre of a hot oven for 30–40 minutes or until loaves shrink slightly from sides of tins and sound hollow when tapped on base, leave to cool on a wire tray.

To freeze bread: Place in a polythene bag. Seal and freeze.

To serve: Allow to thaw for 4 hours at room temperature.

Hot cross buns

Pre-cooking time and oven temperature
15–20 minutes at 425°F., Gas Mark 7

You will need for 12 buns:

1 lb. plain flour	½ teaspoon cinnamon
1 tablespoon dried yeast	½ teaspoon nutmeg
2 oz. castor sugar	2 oz. butter, melted
¼ pint milk	and cooled
¼ pint water	1 egg
1 teaspoon salt	4 oz. currants
½ teaspoon mixed spice	1–2 oz. mixed peel

Glaze:

2 tablespoons milk	1½ oz. sugar
2 tablespoons water	

Place 4 oz. sifted flour in a large mixing bowl. Add yeast and 1 teaspoon sugar. Warm milk and water to about 110°F., add to flour and mix well. Set aside for about 20 minutes until frothy. Sift together remaining flour, salt, mixed spice, cinnamon and nutmeg. Add remaining sugar. Stir butter and egg into risen yeast batter. Add dry ingredients and fruit and mix together; the dough should now be fairly soft. Turn on to a lightly floured board and knead until smooth. Place dough in a lightly greased polythene bag and leave at room temperature until double its original size, about 1½ hours, or overnight in a refrigerator. Divide dough into 12 pieces and shape into round buns. Arrange buns, spaced well apart on floured baking sheets. Place inside lightly greased polythene bags and allow to rise at room temperature for about 30 minutes. Make quick slashes with a very sharp knife or razor, just cutting the surface of the dough to make a cross. Bake in a hot oven for 15–20 minutes.

Bring milk and water to the boil for the glaze. Stir in sugar and boil for a further 2 minutes. Brush hot buns twice with glaze, leave to cool.

To freeze: Place in polythene bags. Seal and freeze.

To serve: Allow to thaw at room temperature for 2–3 hours. See photograph on page 49.

Flower pot loaf

Pre-cooking time and oven temperature
30–40 minutes at 450°F., Gas Mark 8

You will need for 1 loaf:

1 lb. mixed plain flours, wholemeal and white, proportions according to taste	2 teaspoons sugar
	½ pint water
	salt water (optional)
2 teaspoons salt	cracked wheat (optional)
1 oz. fresh yeast or ½ oz. dried yeast	

Do not use plastic flower pot.

Put flours and salt into a bowl. If using fresh yeast, rub into flours, salt and sugar and add all the water. Work to a soft dough, adding more flour if needed, until dough leaves the sides of the bowl clean.

If using dried yeast, add a teaspoon of sugar to half the water at 110°F., and sprinkle dried yeast on top. Leave for 10 minutes or until frothy. Add to flours with remaining sugar and water. Mix to a soft dough and knead on a floured board until smooth.

Place dough in well greased flower pot (see note below) and put inside a large, greased polythene bag, tie loosely. Allow dough to rise until double its original size. Remove bag and, if liked, brush with a little salt water and sprinkle with cracked wheat. Bake, standing upright, in a hot oven for 30–40 minutes. Cool on a rack.

To freeze: Place in a polythene bag. Seal and freeze.

To serve: Allow to thaw at room temperature for 4 hours.

Note: This loaf is baked in a 5-inch top diameter flower pot, which gives the bread a very good texture, in the way the old brick-lined ovens used to. When first using a flower pot for baking, grease it well and bake empty in a hot

oven once or twice. If preferred, the dough can be baked in a loaf tin, or formed into a rough round on a baking sheet.

Walnut streusel loaf

Pre-cooking time and oven temperature
1 hour at 350°F., Gas Mark 4

You will need:

Streusel:

4 oz. demerara sugar	4 oz. walnuts, chopped
1 oz. butter, melted	1 teaspoon cinnamon

Loaf:

4 oz. black treacle	2 oz. butter
¼ pint milk	10 oz. self-raising flour
2 eggs, beaten	4 oz. dates, chopped

Mix ingredients for the streusel together. Blend treacle, milk and beaten eggs. Rub butter into flour and add dates. Lightly mix with liquid. Put half the mixture into a greased and lined 2 lb. loaf tin. Sprinkle over half the streusel, cover with remaining mixture and top with remaining streusel. Bake in a moderate oven for 1 hour. Turn out and cool on a rack.

To freeze: Wrap in moisture-vapour-proof paper or double thickness foil. Seal and freeze.

To serve: Allow to thaw at room temperature for 4 hours.

Short crust pastry

8 oz. pastry means pastry made with 8 oz. flour.

You will need for 2 lb. pastry:

2 lb. plain flour	1 lb. butter, margarine or mixed margarine and lard
1 teaspoon salt	¼ pint water

Sieve together flour and salt. Rub in fat using the tips of the fingers, until mixture resembles fine breadcrumbs. Bind with water to form a firm dough.

To freeze: Divide pastry into two 8 oz. pieces, two 6 oz. pieces and one 4 oz. piece. Wrap in a polythene bag or double thickness foil. Seal and freeze.

To prepare for use: Allow to thaw at room temperature for 1–2 hours, depending on quantity of pastry.

Rough puff pastry

8 oz. pastry means pastry made with 8 oz. flour.

You will need for 2 lb. pastry:

2 lb. plain flour	about 1 pint water
2 teaspoons salt	1 tablespoon lemon juice
1½ lb. butter or margarine	

Sieve together flour and salt. Divide butter or margarine into $\frac{1}{2}$-inch cubes. Add to flour and stir in water and lemon juice. Mix with palette knife until dough clings together. Roll out on a floured board to form an oblong. Mark dough into three and fold lower third up and top third down, like an envelope. Seal edges, refrigerate for 10 minutes. Give dough a half-turn before re-rolling. Repeat rolling and folding 4 times, allowing it to rest in refrigerator for 10 minutes and giving it a half-turn between rollings. Refrigerate for 20 minutes before using.

To freeze: Divide pastry into two 8 oz. pieces, two 6 oz. pieces and one 4 oz. piece. Wrap in a polythene bag or double thickness foil. Seal and freeze.

To prepare for use: Allow to thaw at room temperature for 1–2 hours, depending on quantity of pastry.

Puff pastry

8 oz. pastry means pastry made with 8 oz. flour.

You will need for 2 lb. pastry:

2 lb. plain flour	1 tablespoon lemon juice
2 teaspoons salt	2 lb. butter or margarine
about 1 pint water	

Sieve together flour and salt. Add water and lemon juice and mix to a soft dough. Soften butter or margarine and form into an oblong. Roll out the dough to an oblong about 8 inches by 10 inches. Place butter or margarine on top and fold ends to centre to cover fat. Press centre edges and sides to seal. Give pastry a half-turn and roll out to an oblong. Mark dough into three and fold lower third up and top third down, like an envelope. Seal edges. Give dough a half-turn and leave to rest in refrigerator for 10 minutes. Repeat rolling and folding 6 times, allowing it to rest in refrigerator for 10 minutes between rollings.

To freeze: Divide pastry into two 8 oz. pieces, two 6 oz. pieces and one 4 oz. piece. Wrap in a polythene bag or double thickness foil.

To prepare for use: Allow to thaw at room temperature for 1–2 hours, depending on quantity of pastry.

Hot water crust pastry

8 oz. pastry means pastry made with 8 oz. flour.

You will need for 8 oz. pastry:

8 oz. plain flour	3 oz. lard
$\frac{1}{2}$ teaspoon salt	$\frac{1}{4}$ pint water

Sieve together flour and salt. Put lard and water in saucepan and bring to the boil when lard has melted. Pour into flour and mix with a palette knife until it forms a ball. The pastry must be used while warm or it is very difficult to handle. Keep warm on a board with the hot mixing bowl placed over it, until ready to shape.

To freeze: Wrap in double thickness foil or place in a polythene bag. Seal and freeze.

To prepare for use: Allow to thaw at room temperature for 1–2 hours, depending on quantity of pastry.

Choux pastry

Pre-cooking time   about 5 minutes

You will need for 2-egg quantity choux pastry:

$\frac{1}{4}$ pint water	pinch salt
2 oz. butter	2 eggs
$2\frac{1}{2}$ oz. plain flour	

Put water and butter into a saucepan and bring slowly to the boil. Remove from heat and beat in the flour, sieved with salt, to form a ball which leaves the sides of the pan clean. If necessary, return to a gentle heat. Allow mixture to cool to blood heat, then beat in eggs, one at a time.

To freeze: Wrap in double thickness foil or place in a plastic container and seal.

To prepare for use: Allow to thaw at room temperature for 1–2 hours.

Cheese pastry

8 oz. pastry means pastry made with 8 oz. flour.

You will need for 2 lb. pastry:

2 lb. plain flour	8 oz. strong Cheddar
1 teaspoon salt	cheese, finely grated or
1 teaspoon dry mustard	4 oz. Parmesan cheese,
$\frac{1}{4}$ teaspoon cayenne pepper	finely grated
1 lb. butter or margarine	generous $\frac{1}{4}$ pint water

Sieve together flour, salt, mustard and pepper. Rub in butter or margarine, using the tips of the fingers, until mixture resembles fine breadcrumbs. Add cheese and bind together with water to form a firm dough.

To freeze: Divide pastry into two 8 oz. pieces, two 6 oz. pieces and one 4 oz. piece. Wrap in a polythene bag or double thickness foil. Seal and freeze.

To prepare for use: Allow to thaw at room temperature for 1–2 hours, depending on quantity of pastry.

Chocolate éclairs

Vol-au-vent cases

Pre-cooking time and oven temperature
15–20 minutes at 425°F., Gas Mark 7, then
10 minutes at 400°F., Gas Mark 6
Cooking time and oven temperature, when serving
25 minutes at 375°F., Gas Mark 5

You will need for 8 vol-au-vents:
12 oz. home-made puff   1 egg, beaten with
   pastry (see page 51) or   1 tablespoon water
   2 packets frozen puff
   pastry (13 oz. and 7½ oz.)

Roll out pastry ¼-inch thick. Cut out 16 circles of pastry, using a 3-inch cutter. Place 8 of these on a damp baking tray and brush with egg. Using a 2-inch cutter, stamp out centres of remaining pastry rounds. Put rings on top of bases on baking tray, taking care not to pull them out of shape. Seal well together and brush with egg. Place small circles, for lids, on baking tray and brush with egg. If using home-made pastry, allow to rest in the refrigerator for 20 minutes; this is not necessary for frozen pastry. Bake in a hot oven for 15–20 minutes or until well risen and golden. Remove 'lids', lower heat to moderately hot, and cook for a further 10 minutes. Cool on a rack and remove soft inside from pastry while still warm.
To freeze: When cold, place in a polythene bag, seal and freeze.
To serve: Place on a baking tray while still frozen and reheat in a moderately hot oven for about 25 minutes or until heated through. Fill with hot filling (see page 17).

Chocolate éclairs

Pre-cooking time and oven temperature
25–35 minutes at 400°F., Gas Mark 6
You will need for 14 éclairs:
2-egg quantity choux pastry   few drops vanilla essence
   (see page 51)   6 oz. plain chocolate
¼ pint double cream   1 tablespoon water
1–2 oz. castor sugar

Put pastry into a piping bag with ½-inch plain nozzle and pipe 14 3-inch lengths on greased baking trays. Bake in a moderately hot oven for 25–35 minutes or until crisp and golden. Remove carefully from trays and cool on rack. Lightly whip cream and add sugar and vanilla essence. Make a slit down the side of each éclair and fill with cream, using the piping bag and nozzle if liked. Put chocolate and water into a basin over a pan of hot water, until chocolate has melted. Dip the top of each éclair into the icing and allow to set. See photograph left.
To freeze: Place on a tray and freeze uncovered. When frozen, wrap in double thickness foil or place in a plastic container and seal.
To serve: Unwrap and place on a tray. Allow to thaw at room temperature for 1½ hours.

Baked flan cases

Pre-cooking time and oven temperature
about 17 minutes at 400°F., Gas Mark 6
You will need for four 7–8 inch flans:
1½ lb. short crust pastry (see
   page 50) or 3 packets
   frozen short crust pastry
   (13 oz. sizes)

Divide pastry into four. Roll out each piece and use to line a 7–8-inch flan ring or loose-bottomed sandwich tin. Trim edges, prick bases and chill. Fill centres with crumpled foil or greaseproof paper and baking beans. Bake in a moderately hot oven for about 12 minutes. Remove foil or greaseproof paper and baking beans, and flan rings, but not sandwich tins. Bake for a further 5 minutes to dry out the bases. Cool.
To freeze: Wrap in double thickness foil or polythene bags. Seal and freeze.
To prepare for use: Allow to thaw at room temperature for 1 hour. Use as cases for sweet and savoury flans.

Apple cake (see page 62)

From left to right
Spring soup (see page 67)
Pineapple meringue shortcake (see page 73)
Boeuf à la mode (see page 71)

Blackberry and apple turnovers

French apple slice

Blackberry and apple turnovers

Pre-cooking time and oven temperature
10–15 minutes at 400°F., Gas Mark 6
Cooking time and oven temperature, when serving
30 minutes at 350°F., Gas Mark 4

You will need for 6 servings:

1 packet frozen puff pastry (7½ oz. size) or 4 oz. puff pastry (made with 4 oz. flour)	1 cooking apple, peeled, cored and thinly sliced
4 oz. blackberries	1 oz. castor sugar
	milk
	little extra castor sugar

Roll out pastry very thinly and cut into six 6-inch circles. Mix blackberries, apples and sugar together in a basin, and divide mixture between pastry circles. Moisten edges with milk and fold the pastry over, sealing in the filling well. Brush with a little milk and dust with castor sugar. Place on a baking tray and bake in a moderately hot oven for 10–15 minutes. Cool.
To freeze: Wrap in moisture-vapour-proof paper or double thickness foil. Seal and freeze.
To serve: Either allow to thaw at room temperature for 3–4 hours and serve cold or place while still frozen in a moderate oven for 30 minutes. See photograph on the left.

French apple slice

Pre-cooking time and oven temperature
25 minutes at 425°F., Gas Mark 7

You will need for 6–8 servings:

1 lb. cooking apples, peeled, cored and sliced	1 packet frozen puff pastry (13 oz. size) or 6 oz. puff pastry (made with 6 oz. flour)
1 oz. butter	
1½ oz. sugar	1 egg, beaten with a little milk

Place apples in a pan with butter and sugar. Cook gently, stirring from time to time, until soft. Remove from heat and cool. Roll out pastry to a rectangle 13 inches by 8 inches. Cut in half lengthwise. Place one half on a damp baking tray and spread with cold apple purée to within 1 inch of the edges. Damp edges. Fold second piece of pastry in half lengthwise and cut across the fold at ¼-inch intervals, leaving 1 inch pastry uncut at sides and each end. Lay carefully on top of apple and open out. Seal edges firmly. Brush with egg and milk and bake in a hot oven for 25 minutes. Allow to cool.
To freeze: Wrap in moisture-vapour-proof paper or double thickness foil. Seal and freeze.
To serve: Allow to thaw at room temperature for 5 hours. Dust with icing sugar before serving. See photograph on the left.

Mincemeat medallions

Pre-cooking time and oven temperature
12 minutes at 450°F., Gas Mark 8
Cooking time and oven temperature, when serving
20 minutes at 400°F., Gas Mark 6 or (if uncooked)
30 minutes at 450°F., Gas Mark 8

You will need for 12 medallions:

12 oz. puff pastry or 13 oz. packet frozen puff pastry	1 egg white
	1 teaspoon lemon juice or a few drops of almond essence
3 oz. castor sugar	
3 oz. ground almonds	6 oz. mincemeat

Roll out the puff pastry thinly to make a rectangle 16 inches by 12 inches. Cut into twelve 4-inch squares. Mix the sugar and ground almonds together and add sufficient lightly beaten white of egg to make a soft paste. Flavour with the lemon juice (or a few drops of almond essence if preferred). In the centre of each square put a teaspoon of mincemeat, cover with a dessertspoon of almond mixture. Fold in the four corners to meet at the centre and press down lightly. Arrange the medallions on a damp baking sheet and bake in a hot oven for 12 minutes. Cool quickly.
To freeze: When cold, wrap in heavy-duty foil, seal and freeze. Alternatively, wrap and freeze before baking.
To serve: If already cooked, place on a baking tray and put in a moderately hot oven for 20 minutes or until heated through.
If medallions are uncooked, bake them, while still frozen, in a hot oven for 30 minutes or until pastry is golden brown.

Stuffed duck with orange (see page 72)

Taramasalata and, behind, Country pâté (see recipes page 68)

desserts

On a hot summer day, there is little to equal the taste of a home-made ice-cream or refreshing fruit sorbet. But ices are delicious all the year round, and can be made whenever fruits are at their best and cheapest and stored most successfully in your freezer. Your freezer can also be used to store winter family puddings–crumbles, tarts and pies, even Mince Pies for Christmastime; all freeze well and give an unlimited store of reserve desserts.

If you do not want to tackle the ice-cream recipes, but would still like to stock up with ices, remember that a gallon tin of ice-cream costs far less than the equivalent quantity in small packs. Vanilla and other plain-flavoured ices can be varied by serving with different home-made sauces.

Vanilla ice-cream

You will need for 4 servings:
2 eggs, separated
2 oz. icing sugar, sieved
$\frac{1}{4}$ teaspoon vanilla essence
$\frac{1}{2}$ pint double cream, lightly whipped

Beat egg yolks and 1 oz. icing sugar until thick and creamy. Whisk egg whites until stiff and peaky and gradually beat in remaining sieved icing sugar. Whisk in egg yolks and vanilla essence. Fold in cream.
To freeze: Turn into suitable container. Seal and freeze.
To serve: Allow to thaw a little in a refrigerator for 3 hours before serving. Serve with a little melted chocolate poured over the top. See photograph above right.

Vanilla ice-cream with chocolate sauce

Variations:
Coffee ice-cream: Omit vanilla essence and beat 1 tablespoon coffee essence with egg yolks.
Chocolate ice-cream: Omit vanilla essence and add 2 oz. melted plain chocolate.
Simple cassata: Fold in 1 oz. mixed, chopped candied peel and 1 oz. chopped nuts with the cream.

Orange sorbet

L'orange glacé

You will need for 4 servings:

1 small can evaporated milk
1 can concentrated frozen orange juice (6¼ fl. oz. size)
2 tablespoons Cointreau (optional)

Whisk evaporated milk until thick and fluffy, continue whisking and gradually add the undiluted orange juice and Cointreau, if used. Pour into a container.

To freeze: Cover closely with double thickness foil and freeze.

To serve: Allow to thaw a little in the refrigerator for 3 hours before serving.

Orange ice-cream

You will need for 4 servings:

2 packets cream cheese (3 oz. size)
8 oz. white marshmallows
¼ pint milk
1 can concentrated frozen orange juice (2¾ fl. oz. size)
¼ pint double cream, lightly whipped

Beat cream cheese until light and fluffy. Melt marshmallows with milk in a double saucepan or basin over hot water. Allow to cool. Beat marshmallow mixture into cream cheese gradually. Fold in undiluted orange juice and cream. Pour into container and freeze until lightly set. Remove from container and beat. Return to container, cover closely with double thickness foil and refreeze.

To serve: Allow to thaw a little in a refrigerator for 3 hours before serving.

Lemon sorbet

Pre-cooking time   10 minutes

You will need for 4 servings:

thinly peeled rind and juice 3 lemons
1 pint water
6 oz. loaf sugar
1 egg white

Put lemon rind into a saucepan with water and sugar. Warm over a gentle heat until sugar has dissolved, then boil rapidly for 5–6 minutes. Cool. Add lemon juice and strain into a 1½-pint container. Freeze for about 1 hour or until almost firm. Remove from freezer and mash so that no large lumps remain. Fold in stiffly whisked egg white, cover closely with double thickness foil and refreeze.

To serve: Allow to thaw a little in a refrigerator for 3 hours before serving.

Orange sorbet

You will need for 4 servings:

2 oz. sugar
½ pint water plus 4 tablespoons
¼ oz. gelatine
1 can concentrated frozen orange juice (6¼ fl. oz. size)
1 egg white

Dissolve sugar in ½ pint water, allow to cool. Dissolve gelatine in 4 tablespoons water in a basin over hot water. Add to sugar syrup with undiluted orange juice. Blend well, pour into a 1-pint container and freeze for about 1 hour or until almost firm. Remove from freezer and mash so that no large lumps remain. Fold in stiffly whisked egg white, cover closely with double thickness foil and refreeze.

To serve: Allow to thaw a little in a refrigerator for 3 hours before serving. See photograph on left.

Variation:

Use concentrated grapefruit juice instead of orange.

For a buffet or dinner party: Freeze in a ring mould. Turn out and fill the centre with mandarin orange segments.

Mocha ice-cream charlotte

You will need for 6–8 servings:

4 eggs, separated
4 oz. icing sugar, sieved
4 tablespoons coffee essence
4 tablespoons rum
½ pint double cream, lightly whipped

To serve:
1 packet chocolate finger biscuits

Line sides and bottom of 8-inch cake tin with foil. Whisk egg whites until very stiff, then gradually whisk in icing sugar. Whisk egg yolks, coffee essence and rum together, then gradually whisk into egg whites. Fold in cream.

To freeze: Pour ice-cream mixture into middle of prepared cake tin. Freeze in tin with top tightly covered with foil.

To serve: Carefully remove foil from top, turn out on to serving plate and strip off rest of foil. Arrange chocolate finger biscuits round sides. Allow to thaw a little in a refrigerator for 3 hours before serving.

Ice-cream star cake

Pre-cooking time and oven temperature
20 minutes at 375°F., Gas Mark 5

You will need for 6 servings:

3 oz. self-raising flour	4 oz. castor sugar
1 oz. cocoa powder	2 eggs, beaten
4 oz. butter	$\frac{1}{2}$ teaspoon vanilla essence

Filling:

1 oz. butter	1 oz. glacé cherries,
2 oz. icing sugar, sieved	chopped
few drops vanilla essence	

To serve:

little icing sugar	glacé cherries
vanilla ice-cream	
(family brick)	

Sift together flour and cocoa. Cream butter and sugar until light and fluffy. Gradually beat in eggs, adding a tablespoon of sieved flour and cocoa with the last amount of egg. Beat in vanilla essence. Fold in remaining flour and cocoa. Turn into 2 greased and lined 7-inch sandwich tins. Bake in a moderately hot oven for 20 minutes. Turn out and cool. Cream butter for filling, gradually beat in icing sugar, then add vanilla essence. Stir in chopped glacé cherries. Sandwich chocolate sponges together with filling.
To freeze: Wrap in moisture-vapour-proof paper or double thickness foil. Seal and freeze.
To serve: Allow to thaw at room temperature for 4 hours. Divide cake into 6 wedges. Dust top with icing sugar. Arrange on serving plate with pointed edges of wedges outwards. Pile large spoons of ice-cream from the family block into the centre. Decorate with glacé cherries and serve at once.

Raspberry mousse

You will need for 6 servings:

1 large can evaporated	8 oz. fresh raspberries
milk, chilled	1 raspberry jelly
juice 1 lemon	2 tablespoons water

To serve:
de-frosted raspberries to garnish

Whisk evaporated milk with lemon juice until thick. Sieve raspberries and fold into milk. Put jelly and water in a basin over a pan of simmering water until jelly has dissolved. Allow jelly to cool and fold into mixture.
To freeze: Turn into cake tin, mould or large foil container. Freeze uncovered. When frozen, cover with double thickness foil or moisture-vapour-proof paper.

To serve: Allow to thaw in refrigerator for 24 hours. Turn out and decorate with de-frosted raspberries.

Gooseberry fool

Pre-cooking time   about 25 minutes

You will need for 4 servings:

1$\frac{1}{2}$ lb. gooseberries,	1 tablespoon custard
topped and tailed	powder
2 tablespoons water	$\frac{3}{4}$ pint milk
5 oz. sugar	

Put gooseberries into a pan with water. Cover and cook very gently until soft and pulpy. Sieve, or put in a blender and liquidise. Add sugar and cool. Blend custard powder with 4 tablespoons milk. Bring remaining milk to the boil and pour over blended custard. Return to pan and bring to the boil, stirring all the time until mixture bubbles and thickens. Cover with damp greaseproof paper and allow to cool. Carefully stir gooseberry purée into custard, adding a little extra sugar, if necessary.
To freeze: Turn into serving dish, plastic or other suitable container. Seal and freeze.
To serve: Allow to thaw at room temperature for 6 hours.
Note: If packed in individual plastic containers, these are ideal for picnics. See photograph below.

Gooseberry fool

Mandarin trifle

Pre-cooking time   about 5 minutes

You will need for 4–6 servings:

4–6 trifle sponge cakes	$\frac{1}{2}$ pint milk
2 tablespoons apricot jam	1 tablespoon custard
1 can mandarin oranges	powder
(11 oz. size)	1 oz. sugar
3 tablespoons sherry	$\frac{1}{4}$ pint double cream,
(optional)	lightly whipped

Split sponge cakes in half and spread with jam.
Sandwich together and place in the base of a
serving dish or plastic container. Strain juice
from mandarins and pour over sponges, together with sherry, if used, and leave to soak.
Scatter mandarins on top, leaving a few for
decoration. Blend 4 tablespoons milk with
custard powder and sugar. Bring remaining
milk to the boil and pour over blended custard.
Return to pan and bring to the boil, stirring all
the time until sauce bubbles and thickens. Pour
over mandarins and leave to cool. Lightly whip
cream and pipe or spread over custard. Arrange
mandarin segments on top.

To freeze: Cover closely with foil or lid. Seal
and freeze.

To serve: Allow to thaw at room temperature
for 4–6 hours.

Cinnamon and almond slices

Pre-cooking time and oven temperature
20 minutes at 350°F., Gas Mark 4

You will need for 18 biscuits:

4 oz. butter	1 egg, beaten
2 oz. castor sugar	1 oz. flaked almonds
6 oz. plain flour	$\frac{1}{2}$ oz. granulated sugar
$\frac{1}{2}$ teaspoon cinnamon	

Cream butter and castor sugar together until
light and fluffy. Add sifted flour and cinnamon
and work well together. Press into a buttered
7-inch by 11-inch Swiss roll tin and flatten with
a knife. Brush with a little beaten egg and prick
with a fork. Sprinkle almonds and granulated
sugar over the top. Bake in a moderate oven for
20 minutes or until golden brown. Mark into
18 fingers while still warm. Cool in the tin.

To freeze: Remove from tin and cut into fingers.
Wrap in double thickness foil or polythene bag.
Seal and freeze.

To serve: Allow to thaw at room temperature
for 5 hours.

Gâteau Diane

Pre-cooking time and oven temperature
about 6 hours at 225°F., Gas Mark $\frac{1}{4}$

You will need for 12 servings:

6 eggs, separated	7$\frac{1}{2}$ fl. oz. water
12 oz. castor sugar	(12 tablespoons)
9 oz. plain chocolate	1 can pineapple pieces
12 oz. unsalted butter	(16 oz. size)
6 oz. loaf or granulated sugar	

To serve:
glacé pineapple pieces

Mark out three 8-inch circles on greased, greaseproof paper or parchment paper. Whisk egg
whites until stiff and peaky. Whisk in half the
castor sugar a teaspoon at a time and fold in
remainder. Divide mixture between circles,
spreading out to the edges. Bake in a very slow
oven for about 6 hours or until meringue is hard.
Remove from oven and cool.

Melt chocolate in a basin over hot water and beat
into creamed butter. Lightly beat egg yolks. Put
loaf or granulated sugar with water in a saucepan over a gentle heat until sugar has dissolved.
Boil to 230°F., or until syrup forms a long
thread when dropped into a basin of cold water.
Gradually beat into egg yolks, then add this
slowly to butter mixture. Drain pineapple pieces
and chop. Spread a thin layer of chocolate icing
and half the pineapple on two rounds of
meringue. Pile one of these meringues on top of
the other and top with third meringue. Cover
completely with remaining chocolate mixture.

To freeze: Wrap in double thickness foil and
freeze.

To serve: Allow to thaw at room temperature
for 6 hours. Mark all over the icing with a fork
to decorate and top with glacé pineapple pieces
if liked. Thaw unwrapped.

Florida cheesecake

You will need for 4 servings:

Biscuit crust:

2 oz. butter	1 oz. castor sugar
4 oz. digestive biscuits, crushed with a rolling pin	

Filling:

2 eggs, separated	8 oz. cottage cheese
2 oz. castor sugar	½ pint double cream, lightly whipped
1½ tablespoons concentrated frozen orange juice	

Melt butter and stir in biscuits and sugar. Mix well. Line an 8-inch sandwich tin with double thickness foil. Press biscuit mixture into tin with a spoon, leave in a refrigerator to set. Beat egg yolks and sugar together in a bowl over hot water until thick and creamy. Add undiluted orange juice. Allow to cool. Mash the cheese with a fork and add to the mixture. Fold in cream and stiffly beaten egg whites. Pour into prepared sandwich tin.

To freeze: Fold over foil. Seal and freeze. When frozen remove from tin.

To serve: Allow to thaw at room temperature for 1 hour. Serve semi-frozen.

Apricot cheesecake

You will need for 12 servings:

2 orange jellies	½ pint double cream, lightly whipped
1 can apricots (1 lb. 12 oz. size)	8 oz. ginger biscuits, lightly crushed with a rolling pin
1½ lb. cottage cheese, sieved	
1½ oz. castor sugar	2 oz. soft brown sugar
	3 oz. butter, melted

Dissolve jelly in a basin over hot water with 6 tablespoons apricot juice. Chop or sieve drained apricots and add to sieved cottage cheese with castor sugar. Stir in cooled jelly. Carefully fold in whipped cream when mixture is thick, but not set. Turn into 10-inch cake tin and leave to set. Mix crushed ginger biscuits with sugar and butter. Sprinkle over top of cheesecake and press down lightly.

To freeze: Cover with double thickness foil or moisture-vapour-proof paper. Seal and freeze.

To serve: Allow to thaw in the refrigerator for 24 hours. Turn out and decorate with apricot halves (from 1 lb. 12 oz. can). Brush with apricot glaze, made from 3 tablespoons sieved apricot jam and 1 tablespoon water and sprinkle with flaked, browned almonds. See colour photograph on page 44.

Apple cake

Pre-cooking time and oven temperature
1 hour at 325°F., Gas Mark 3

You will need:

7 oz. self-raising flour	12 oz. large cooking apples
pinch salt	lemon juice
5 oz. butter	2 tablespoons sugar
3 oz. castor sugar	2 tablespoons apricot jam
1 egg, beaten	

To serve:

little icing sugar	slices of dessert apple

Sieve together flour and salt. Cream butter and sugar together until light and fluffy and beat in the egg. Fold in sifted flour and salt. Spread three-quarters of the mixture over the bottom of a greased and lined 7–8-inch cake tin. Peel, core and slice the apples and squeeze lemon juice over to preserve the colour. Arrange overlapping slices on the cake mixture and sprinkle with the sugar. Heat the apricot jam and brush over the apples. Take small pieces of the remaining mixture, roll into strips with floured hands and arrange a lattice pattern over the apples. Put into a moderate oven and bake for 1 hour.

To freeze: Turn out and allow to cool on a wire rack. When cold, wrap in double thickness foil or moisture-vapour-proof paper. Seal and freeze.

To serve: Allow to thaw at room temperature for about 4 hours. Reheat in a moderate oven if desired. Serve dusted with icing sugar and decorated with slices of fresh dessert apple. See colour photograph on page 53.

Farmhouse apple pie

Cooking time and oven temperature, when serving
1 hour at 400°F., Gas Mark 6

You will need for 4 servings:

1½ lb. cooking apples	6 oz. short crust pastry (see page 50) or 1 packet frozen short crust pastry (7½ oz. size)
3 oz. soft brown sugar	
1 oz. butter	
3 cloves	
¼ teaspoon cinnamon	

Peel apples and slice thinly. Place in pie dish in layers with sugar, butter, cloves and cinnamon. Roll out pastry and use to top pie. Knock up the edges with the back of a knife and flute edges.

To freeze: Freeze uncovered. When frozen place in a polythene bag or wrap in double thickness foil. Seal and freeze.

To serve: Brush with milk and sprinkle with castor sugar. While still frozen bake in a moderately hot oven for 1 hour.

Treacle tart

Pre-cooking time and oven temperature
30 minutes at 400°F., Gas Mark 6
Cooking time and oven temperature, when serving
30 minutes at 350°F., Gas Mark 4

You will need for 4–6 servings:

6 oz. short crust pastry (see | 2 oz. white breadcrumbs
(page 50) or 1 packet | 1 teaspoon lemon juice
frozen short crust pastry | little milk
(7½ oz. size)
6 tablespoons golden syrup

Roll out pastry thinly and use to line a deep 8-inch plate. Warm the syrup and mix with the breadcrumbs and lemon juice. Spread syrup mixture over pastry. Roll out pastry trimmings and cut narrow strips for lattice and arrange on tart. To decorate edge, make 1-inch cuts in the pastry round the edge at 1-inch intervals. Brush with milk and fold each inch square of pastry over to form triangles round the edge. Bake in a moderately hot oven for 30 minutes. Allow to cool.
To freeze: Wrap in a polythene bag, double thickness foil or moisture-vapour-proof paper. Seal and freeze.
To serve: If serving cold, allow to thaw at room temperature for 5 hours. If serving hot, bake in a moderate oven for 30 minutes.

Plum and orange crumble

Pre-cooking time and oven temperature
1½ hours at 325°F., Gas Mark 3
Cooking time and oven temperature, when serving
40 minutes at 400°F., Gas Mark 6

You will need for 4 servings:

1½ lb. plums, stoned | 8 oz. plain flour
about 3 oz. soft brown | 4 oz. butter
sugar | 2 oz. castor sugar
grated rind and juice
of 1 orange

Put stoned plums into an ovenproof dish or large foil dish. Sprinkle with sugar, (the amount will depend on the sweetness of the plums) and pour over orange juice. Sieve flour and rub in butter until mixture resembles fine breadcrumbs. Add sugar and grated orange rind. Sprinkle over the plums and press down lightly. Bake in a moderate oven for 1½ hours. Cool quickly.
To freeze: Cover closely with double thickness foil. Seal and freeze.
To serve: Place while still frozen in a moderately hot oven for about 40 minutes or until heated through.

Mince pies

Pre-cooking time and oven temperature
25 minutes at 400°F., Gas Mark 6
Cooking time and oven temperature, when serving
15 minutes at 350°F., Gas Mark 4

You will need for 12 mince pies:

8 oz. short crust pastry | 12 oz. mincemeat
(see page 50)

Roll out pastry thinly and cut 12 circles using a 3¼-inch fluted cutter and 12 circles using a 2¾-inch fluted cutter. Place large circles in patty tins and prick bases with a fork. Put a heaped teaspoon of mincemeat on each. Moisten the edges of the pastry with water and top with a smaller circle of pastry. Bake for about 25 minutes in a moderately hot oven or until golden brown.
To freeze: Cool, wrap in polythene bags. Seal and freeze.
To serve: Reheat while still frozen in a moderate oven for about 15 minutes.
Note: If preferred, the pies can be frozen before baking. Freeze in patty tins and when frozen, remove from tins, pack into polythene bags and and seal. Bake while still frozen in a hot oven for about 35 minutes until golden.

Oranges in caramel sauce

Pre-cooking time   about 20 minutes

You will need for 12 servings:

15 medium sized oranges | 1¼ pints water
12 oz. sugar

Remove pith and skin from 12 oranges and cut into ¼-inch slices. Squeeze juice from remaining 3 oranges. Put sugar into a strong pan over a moderate heat. Stir until sugar has melted and turned a caramel colour. Draw to one side of the stove and very gradually add the water. Be very careful as the caramel will boil furiously. Return pan to the heat and stir gently until caramel has dissolved. Remove from heat, add strained orange juice and leave to cool. Pour over oranges.
To freeze: Turn into a plastic or other suitable container. Seal and freeze.
To serve: Allow to thaw in a refrigerator for 24 hours. Serve chilled with Cinnamon and Almond Slices (see page 61). A little orange liqueur can be added if liked.

Vanilla sauce

Pre-cooking time   5 minutes

You will need for two 4 servings:
1 oz. cornflour   1 pint milk
2 oz. sugar   1 teaspoon vanilla essence

Blend cornflour and sugar with a little of the milk. Heat remaining milk in a pan to boiling point. Pour over cornflour, stirring. Return mixture to pan and bring to the boil, stirring all the time until sauce bubbles and thickens. Add vanilla essence.

To freeze: Divide between two plastic or other suitable containers, leaving ½-inch headspace. Cover with a circle of damp greaseproof paper and cool quickly. Seal and freeze.

To serve: Allow to thaw at room temperature for 4 hours. Remove greaseproof paper and re-heat gently, beating from time to time.

Variations:

Coffee sauce: Omit vanilla and add 2 table-spoons coffee essence.

Chocolate sauce: Omit vanilla essence and blend 2 tablespoons cocoa powder and 2 oz. extra sugar with cornflour. Add 1 oz. butter to thickened sauce.

Butterscotch sauce: Omit vanilla essence. Put 2 oz. butter and 8 oz. brown sugar into a pan and heat gently until butter has melted. Add to thickened sauce.

Chestnut stuffing   *Bread sauce* *Sausage meat stuffing*   *Cranberry sauce*

entertaining

When it comes to entertaining, your freezer is a true friend. You can cook ahead, including intricate decorations for a party sweet, and even make canapés to serve with drinks, all at your leisure – an afternoon earlier in the week, perhaps, or even a month ahead of the party. When party-day comes round, you will be able to relax and talk to your guests properly without frantic last-minute dashes out to the kitchen to whip cream, make gravy or do any other small but time-consuming task.

Elaborate dishes, when frozen unwrapped, become quite solid and easy to handle. They can then be wrapped for longer freezing without fear of damage, defrosted when required and – as if by magic – there is your dinner party dish! Our Pineapple Meringue Shortcake (see page 73) is a perfect example. It looks so fragile but once frozen there is no danger at all of its being damaged.

Chestnut stuffing

Pre-cooking time   30 minutes

You will need to stuff the front of a 12 lb. turkey:

1 lb. chestnuts	1 large egg, beaten
stock	2 oz. butter, melted
4 oz. brown breadcrumbs	salt and pepper
grated rind of $\frac{1}{2}$ lemon	

Make a slit in each chestnut with a sharp knife. Cook in boiling water for 5 minutes, then peel. Return to pan with stock so that the chestnuts are just covered. Simmer for about 20 minutes or until tender. Drain thoroughly, then sieve or put into a blender. Mix with breadcrumbs and lemon rind. Beat in egg and butter and season to taste. See photograph on page 64.
To freeze: Pack into a plastic container or polythene bag. Seal and freeze.

To prepare for use: Allow to thaw in the refrigerator for 24 hours. Use to stuff the neck end of the turkey.

Sausage meat stuffing

Pre-cooking time   5 minutes

You will need to stuff the back of a 12 lb. turkey:

3 oz. lamb's liver or	3 tablespoons chopped
2 oz. lamb's liver and	parsley
the turkey liver	1$\frac{1}{2}$ teaspoons dried thyme
1 oz. butter	grated rind and juice
12 oz. pork sausage meat	$\frac{1}{2}$ lemon
1 onion, finely chopped	salt and pepper
8 oz. white breadcrumbs	1 egg, beaten

Chop liver finely and fry in butter for 5 minutes. Add to remaining ingredients and mix well. See photograph on page 64.
To freeze: Pack into a plastic container or polythene bag. Seal and freeze.
To prepare for use: Allow to thaw in the refrigerator for 24 hours. Use to stuff the main cavity of the turkey.
Note: Make sure the sausage meat is fresh.

Cranberry sauce

Pre-cooking time   15 minutes

You will need for $\frac{3}{4}$ pint sauce:

8 oz. cranberries	$\frac{1}{4}$ pint water
4 oz. sugar	

Put cranberries, sugar and water into a saucepan and cook over a gentle heat for 15 minutes.
To freeze: Cool quickly. Turn into a plastic or other suitable container. See photograph on page 64. Seal and freeze.
To serve: Allow to thaw in the refrigerator for 15 hours. Reheat gently.

French onion soup

Gazpacho

You will need for 6 servings:

2 lb. tomatoes	2 tablespoons wine
2 cloves garlic	vinegar
1 green pepper	$\frac{1}{4}$ pint chicken stock
1 medium sized onion	6 tablespoons olive oil
$\frac{1}{2}$ cucumber	salt and pepper
4 oz. fresh white or	
brown breadcrumbs	

To serve:
croûtons of fried bread

Peel tomatoes. Either put tomatoes, garlic, pepper and unpeeled cucumber into a blender and liquidise, or rub tomatoes through a sieve, crush garlic and chop pepper, onion and cucumber very finely. Add breadcrumbs, vinegar and stock. Gradually beat in oil. Season well with salt and pepper.

To freeze: Pour into a plastic or other suitable container, leaving 1-inch headspace. Seal and freeze.

To serve: Allow to thaw in refrigerator for 24 hours. Serve chilled and dilute to taste with extra stock, ice cubes and croûtons of fried bread.

Bread sauce

Pre-cooking time   5 minutes

you will need for $\frac{1}{2}$ pint sauce:

1 onion	2 oz. white breadcrumbs
2 cloves	salt and pepper
$\frac{1}{2}$ pint milk	$\frac{1}{2}$ oz. butter

Put onion, with the cloves inserted, into a pan with milk. Heat gently to boiling point, then turn off the heat and leave to infuse for 30 minutes. Remove onion and cloves and stir in breadcrumbs, seasoning and butter.

To freeze: Cool quickly. Turn into a plastic or other suitable container. See photograph on page 64. Seal and freeze.

To serve: Allow to thaw in the refrigerator for 12 hours. Reheat very gently to boiling point.

French onion soup

Pre-cooking time   1 hour

You will need for 12 servings:

6 oz. butter
9 large onions,
    finely chopped

3 pints water
6 beef stock cubes
salt and pepper

To serve:

toasted French bread   grated cheese

Melt butter in pan, add onions, cover pan and cook very gently for about 45 minutes. Remove from heat and add water. Bring to boil slowly, crumble in stock cubes and season to taste with salt and pepper. Simmer gently for 10 minutes.
To freeze: Cool quickly. Pour into plastic or other suitable containers, leaving 1-inch headspace. Seal and freeze.
To serve: Allow to thaw at room temperature for 8 hours. Reheat gently to boiling point. Serve topped with slices of toasted French bread, covered with cheese and browned under grill.

Spring soup

Pre-cooking time   30 minutes

You will need for 12 servings:

3 oz. butter
1 lettuce, chopped
2 bunches watercress,
    chopped
2 bunches spring onions,
    chopped

$1\frac{1}{2}$ pints water
2 chicken stock cubes
$1\frac{1}{2}$ pints milk
salt and freshly milled
    black pepper

To serve:

$\frac{1}{2}$ pint single cream   watercress to garnish

Melt butter in a large pan and add lettuce, watercress and spring onions. Cook over a gentle heat, with the lid on, for about 10 minutes to soften the vegetables. Remove from heat, add water, crumble in stock cubes and add milk. Season well with salt and pepper. Return to heat, bring to boil, then simmer gently for about 15 minutes or until vegetables are tender. Strain off liquid and sieve vegetables, adding the purée to the liquor, or put the mixture into a blender and liquidise.
To freeze: Cool quickly. Pour into plastic or other suitable containers, leaving 1-inch headspace. Seal and freeze.
To serve: If serving cold, allow to thaw in refrigerator for 24 hours and stir in $\frac{1}{2}$ pint single cream when thawed. If serving hot, allow to thaw at room temperature for 8 hours. Reheat gently and bring to the boil. Remove from heat and stir in $\frac{1}{2}$ pint single cream. Turn into soup tureen or bowls without further heating. Garnish with watercress. See colour photograph page 53.

Pea soup

Pre-cooking time   40 minutes

You will need for 4 servings:

6 large lettuce leaves,
    washed
1 bunch spring onions
2 oz. butter

1 lb. shelled peas
2 tablespoons water
salt and pepper

To serve:

1 pint chicken stock or
    water and stock cubes

$\frac{1}{4}$ pint single cream

Shred lettuce leaves and roughly chop onions. Melt butter in a pan and add all the other ingredients. Cover and cook over a gentle heat shaking the pan from time to time, for 40 minutes or until peas are tender. Sieve or put into a blender.
To freeze: Cool quickly. Turn into a plastic or other suitable container. Seal and freeze.
To serve: Allow to thaw at room temperature for 4 hours. Reheat gently with 1 pint chicken stock or water and stock cubes. Adjust seasoning and stir in $\frac{1}{4}$ pint single cream just before serving.

Liver pâté

Pre-cooking time and oven temperature
$1\frac{1}{2}$ hours at 350°F., Gas Mark 4

You will need for 6 servings:

4 oz. pig's liver
4 oz. fat bacon, with rind
    cut off
1 small onion, chopped
1 small clove garlic,
    chopped
2 oz. butter
$\frac{1}{2}$ teaspoon anchovy essence

1 teaspoon made mustard
$\frac{1}{4}$ pint milk
1 blade mace
1 bay leaf
2–3 peppercorns
$\frac{1}{2}$ oz. butter
$\frac{1}{2}$ oz. flour
salt and pepper

Gently fry liver, bacon, onion and garlic in butter for about 10 minutes. Then put into a blender and liquidise, or put through a mincer. Add anchovy essence and mustard. Put milk in a saucepan with mace, bay leaf and peppercorns. Bring very slowly to the boil and leave for 5 minutes. Strain. Melt butter in pan, add flour and cook for 1 minute. Remove from heat and gradually stir in milk. Return to heat and bring to boil, stirring all the time until the mixture bubbles and thickens. Blend with meat mixture and season to taste. Turn into a well-greased 1 pint terrine, cover with foil or lid. Stand in a roasting tin of hot water and bake in a moderate oven for 1 hour.
To freeze: Cool quickly. Turn out of dish, wrap in double or heavy-duty foil and freeze.
To serve: Allow to thaw in refrigerator for 8 hours.

Country pâté

Pre-cooking time and oven temperature
1½–2 hours at 325°F., Gas Mark 3

You will need for 6–8 servings:

1 bay leaf	¼ teaspoon dried dill
3 or 4 rashers streaky bacon	¼ teaspoon ground mace
1 lb. chicken livers	1½ teaspoons salt
8 oz. bacon trimmings	¼ teaspoon freshly milled
1 large onion	black pepper
1 clove garlic	4 tablespoons port
2 teaspoons made mustard	1 egg, beaten
¼ teaspoon mixed herbs	1 tablespoon instant
¼ teaspoon dried thyme	potato powder

Butter a 2 pint terrine or straight-sided dish and place the bay leaf in the bottom. Cover with streaky bacon, stretched on a board with the back of a knife. Mince chicken livers, bacon trimmings, onion and garlic. Add seasonings, port, egg and potato powder, mix well. Turn into terrine or dish and cover with foil or lid. Place in a roasting tin of hot water and bake in a moderate oven for 1½–2 hours.
To freeze: Cool quickly. Turn out of dish, wrap in double thickness foil and freeze.
To serve: Allow to thaw in refrigerator for 24 hours. See colour photograph on page 56.

Pork terrine

Pre-cooking time and oven temperature
2½ hours at 350°F., Gas Mark 4

You will need for 12 servings:

6–8 rashers streaky bacon	8 oz. bacon trimmings
1 bay leaf	1 lb. pig's liver
4 slices crustless white	1 large onion
bread	2 cloves garlic
2 eggs	½ teaspoon mixed herbs
about ¼ pint milk	2 teaspoons salt
12 oz. streaky pork	½ teaspoon pepper

Well grease a 2½ pint terrine or loaf tin. Remove rinds from streaky bacon and flatten and stretch rashers with the blade of a knife. Place bay leaf in bottom of dish and arrange the rashers over it and round the sides. Mash bread to a soft pulp with eggs and milk. Remove rind from pork and bacon trimmings and chop finely or mince, with liver, onion and garlic. Mix well with bread and season with herbs and salt and pepper. Turn into prepared dish, cover tightly with foil or lid. Place dish in roasting tin of hot water. Bake in a moderate oven for about 2½ hours.
To freeze: Cool quickly. Turn out of dish, wrap in double thickness foil and freeze.
To serve: Allow to thaw in refrigerator for 24 hours.

Taramasalata

You will need for 6 servings:

3 oz. crustless white bread	¼ pint olive oil
water	juice ½ lemon
8 oz. smoked cod's roe	freshly milled black pepper
1 small clove garlic,	
crushed	

To serve:
black olives to garnish

Soak bread in water for a few minutes. When soft, squeeze out as much water as possible. Pound bread, roe and garlic together, or put in a blender and liquidise. Beat in half the oil a drop at a time, add the lemon juice and the remaining oil. Season to taste with pepper.
To freeze: Form into a square on a piece of double thickness foil. Seal and freeze.
To serve: Allow to thaw in refrigerator for 24 hours. Make a criss-cross pattern on top with a knife, or pipe into small dishes and decorate with black olives. Serve with hot toast or French bread. See colour photograph on page 56.

Potato croquettes

Pre-cooking time   about 25 minutes
Cooking time, when serving
5 or 10 minutes

You will need for 6 servings:

1½ lb. potatoes	3 eggs
salt and pepper	browned breadcrumbs
2 oz. butter	

Cook peeled and halved potatoes in boiling, salted water until tender. Strain and mash with butter. Beat in a whole, beaten egg and one egg yolk. Season with salt and pepper. Form potato into 18 small, cork-shaped croquettes. Beat remaining egg white and whole egg with 2 tablespoons water and strain. Dip croquettes in beaten egg and roll in breadcrumbs.
To freeze: Pack into a plastic container or wrap in double thickness foil. Seal and freeze.
To serve: Deep fry in oil or lard at a temperature in which a day-old cube of bread turns brown in 1 minute. If croquettes are still frozen, fry for about 10 minutes; if thawed for about 5 minutes.

Moussaka

Moussaka

Pre-cooking time   about 45 minutes
Cooking time and oven temperature, when serving
1½ hours at 350°F., Gas Mark 4

You will need for 12 servings:

6 large aubergines	1 teaspoon mixed, dried
salt	herbs
scant ¼ pint oil	3 tablespoons chopped
3 lb. onions, chopped	parsley
2 cloves garlic, crushed	2 oz. butter
or very finely chopped	3 oz. flour
3 lb. boned shoulder	1½ pints milk
lamb, coarsely minced	2 teaspoons made mustard
2 oz. flour	12 oz. strong Cheddar
pepper	cheese, grated
1 can tomatoes (1¾ lb. size)	

Slice unpeeled aubergines in ½-inch rounds.
Sprinkle with salt and leave for 30 minutes;
drain. Wash and dry. Fry aubergines, using as
little oil as possible; lift on to kitchen paper. Add
remaining oil and fry onions, garlic and meat
for about 15 minutes. Blend in flour, seasoning,
tomato juice from can, herbs and parsley. Bring
to the boil, stirring all the time. Melt butter in
pan, add flour and cook for a few minutes.
Remove from heat and gradually stir in milk.
Return to heat and bring to the boil, stirring all
the time until mixture bubbles and thickens.
Stir in mustard, cheese and seasoning.

To freeze: In 2 ovenproof dishes, arrange layers
of aubergine, meat mixture and tomato, finish-
ing with aubergine slices. Pour over cheese
sauce and cool quickly. Cover closely with
double thickness foil. Seal and freeze.

To serve: Bake while still frozen in a moderate
oven for 1½ hours. Serve hot with French bread
and butter, and salad. See photograph above.

Note: 2 lb. potatoes can be substituted for the
aubergines; cook potatoes until just tender, then
slice and use as above.

Salmon and crab rolls

Spicy risotto

Pre-cooking time   about 45 minutes
Cooking time and oven temperature, when serving
45 minutes at 350°F., Gas Mark 4

You will need for 12 servings:

8 oz. butter	5 chicken stock cubes
6 onions, chopped	or use 3 pints Chicken
4 cloves garlic, crushed	stock (see page 22)
or very finely chopped	$1\frac{1}{2}$ lb. frozen peas
$1\frac{3}{4}$ lb. rice	$1\frac{1}{2}$ lb. cooked ham, chicken
2–3 tablespoons curry	or pork, chopped
powder	salt and pepper
3 pints water	

Melt butter in a large saucepan and fry onion and garlic for about 10 minutes or until golden. Add rice and fry for 5 minutes. Stir in curry powder and water, crumble in stock cubes, or stir in curry powder and stock. Bring to the boil, cover and simmer gently for about 15 minutes. Stir in peas and meat and a little extra water, if necessary, and cook for a further 5 minutes or until peas are cooked. Season to taste.
To freeze: Cool quickly. Pack into large polythene bag(s) or other suitable container(s). Seal and freeze.
To serve: Allow to thaw at room temperature for 8 hours. Place in a large roasting tin, cover with foil and make a few holes in the foil with a fork to allow the steam to escape. Reheat in a moderate oven for about 45 minutes, or until heated through, stirring lightly with a fork from time to time.

Salmon and crab rolls

You will need for 24 rolls:

3 oz. butter	2 tablespoons mayonnaise
1 small brown loaf, sliced	lemon juice
8 oz. smoked salmon	salt and freshly milled
1 can crab meat	black pepper
(6 oz. size)	

To serve:
watercress to garnish

Butter 12 slices of bread. Remove crusts and cut each slice in half. Divide salmon into 24 small equal pieces. Drain and flake crab meat. Mix with mayonnaise, lemon juice and seasoning. Place a small amount of crab on each piece of salmon and roll up. Place on top of bread.
To freeze: Place on a flat tray, Wrap in moisture-vapour-proof paper or double thickness foil. Seal and freeze.
To serve: Allow to thaw, covered in refrigerator for 12 hours. Serve garnished with watercress See photograph above.

Chicken and ham pancakes

Pre-cooking time   1 hour
Cooking time and oven temperature, when serving
20 minutes at 375°F., Gas Mark 5

You will need for 12 servings:
Pancakes:

12 oz. flour	1½ pints milk
¾ teaspoon salt	3 tablespoons oil
3 eggs, beaten	lard for frying
3 egg yolks	

Filling:

3 oz. butter	½ pint milk
3 oz. flour	1 lb. cooked chicken,
½ pint chicken or ham	chopped
stock or water and	8 oz. cooked ham,
stock cube	chopped
½ pint dry cider	salt and pepper

Sieve flour and salt into a bowl. Make a well in
the centre and drop in beaten eggs and egg yolks.
Add half the milk and mix to a smooth batter.
Beat well, then add remaining milk and oil. Melt
a little lard in an 8-inch pan and heat until hot.
Using a ladle, pour in batter until it covers the
base of the pan thinly. Cook until underside is
golden. Turn or toss pancake and fry until
second side is cooked. Turn out of pan on to a
clean tea towel. Repeat with remaining batter.
This quantity of batter makes 24 pancakes.
Filling: Melt butter, add flour and cook for 3
minutes. Remove from heat and gradually add
stock and cider. Return to heat and bring to the
boil, stirring all the time until sauce bubbles and
thickens, then stir in milk. Add meat and season.
To freeze: Stack pancakes one on top of each
other, with a circle of greaseproof paper between
each. Wrap in double thickness foil, moisture-
vapour-proof paper or polythene bags. Seal and
freeze. Cool filling quickly and turn into a
plastic or other container. Seal and freeze.
To serve: Allow pancakes to thaw at room
temperature for 8 hours and filling for 12 hours.
Divide filling among pancakes and roll up. Place
on an ovenproof dish, cover with foil and reheat
in a moderately hot oven for 20 minutes.

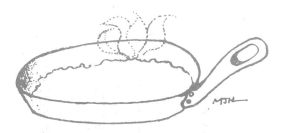

Boeuf à la mode

Pre-cooking time and oven temperature
about 3 hours at 325°F., Gas Mark 3
Cooking time and oven temperature, when serving
40 minutes at 325°F., Gas Mark 3

You will need for 6 servings:

3 lb. rolled topside of beef	6 oz. fat bacon, cut in
2 large carrots, sliced	1-inch cubes
1 large onion, sliced	2 pints beef stock or
1 clove garlic, crushed	2 pints water and
1 bouquet garni	2 stock cubes
6 peppercorns	1 calf's foot, cleaned
1 teaspoon mixed spice	and skinned
¾ pint red wine	salt and pepper

Put meat into a large bowl with carrots, onion,
garlic, bouquet garni, peppercorns, mixed spice
and wine. Leave in the marinade for at least 12
hours, turning from time to time. Remove meat
and dry with kitchen paper. Put bacon into a
saucepan or fireproof casserole, heat and when
sufficient fat has run out, add meat and brown
quickly on all sides. Pour off any excess fat. Add
marinade, stock, calf's foot and seasoning to meat.
Simmer very gently for about 3 hours on top of
the stove or in a moderate oven. Remove meat
from pan, skim off any excess fat and reduce
liquid to about 1 pint. Strain.
To freeze: Cool quickly. Pack meat and sauce,
together with chopped meat from calf's foot,
into a waxed carton or other suitable container.
Seal and freeze.
To serve: Allow to thaw at room temperature
for 8 hours. Reheat gently in a moderate oven
for 40 minutes. Serve with button onions and
new carrots. See colour photograph on page 53.

Boeuf bourguignonne

Pre-cooking time   3 hours

You will need for 6 servings:

6 oz. piece flank bacon	1½ oz. flour
2 lb. stewing steak, cut	¾ pint water
into 1½-inch cubes	¾ pint red wine
12 oz. carrots, peeled	2 beef stock cubes
and sliced	1 bouquet garni
12 small onions, peeled	salt and pepper
2 cloves garlic, pressed	4 oz. button mushrooms
or very finely chopped	

Remove rind from bacon and cut into ½-inch
pieces. Fry over a low heat until the fat runs out.
Increase heat, add steak, carrots, onions and
garlic and cook for about 15 minutes or until
meat is evenly browned, stirring from time to
time. Stir in flour and cook for 5 minutes.
Gradually stir in water and wine. Bring to the

boil, stirring occasionally. Add stock cubes, bouquet garni and seasoning. If the bacon is very salty, do not add any more salt. Cover and simmer for 2½ hours or until meat is tender. Add mushrooms 15 minutes before end of cooking time.

To freeze: Cool quickly. Turn into a plastic or other suitable container. Seal and freeze.

To serve: Allow to thaw at room temperature for 8 hours. Reheat gently in a saucepan.

Casserole of pheasant

Pre-cooking time and oven temperature
2¼–4¼ hours at 325°F., Gas Mark 3
Cooking time and oven temperature, when serving
30 minutes at 325°F., Gas Mark 3

You will need for 6 servings:

1 tablespoon oil	1 tablespoon redcurrant
1 oz. butter	jelly
1 old pheasant	¼ pint port
2 medium sized onions,	1 bay leaf
thinly sliced	sprig parsley
2 oz. flour	salt and pepper
¾ pint stock	
thinly peeled rind and	
juice 1 orange	

To serve:
orange slices to garnish

Heat oil, add butter and fry pheasant quickly until it is a good golden colour. Remove from pan and place in 2½ pint casserole. Add onions to fat in pan, fry till soft and golden brown. Stir in flour and continue to cook for a few minutes until it is brown. Blend in stock, bring to the boil, simmer for 2–3 minutes, stirring all the time. Add orange rind and juice, redcurrant jelly, port, bay leaf and parsley. Simmer until jelly has dissolved, add salt and pepper to taste. Pour over pheasant, cover and cook in a moderate oven for 2–4 hours, depending on the size and age of the bird.

To freeze: Cool quickly. Divide into joints or remove meat from bone and cut into 1-inch pieces. Turn into plastic or other suitable container, leaving ½-inch headspace. Seal and freeze.

To serve: Allow to thaw at room temperature for 8 hours. Reheat gently in a moderate oven for 30 minutes. Serve, garnished with orange slices.

Stuffed duck with orange

Cooking time and oven temperature, when serving
1½ hours at 375°F., Gas Mark 5

You will need for 6 servings:

1 duck, about 5 lb.	4 oz. fresh white
salt and pepper	breadcrumbs
1 large onion, chopped	2 oranges
1 oz. butter	¼ teaspoon mixed herbs
1 lb. chicken livers	1 egg, beaten
6 oz. streaky pork	

To serve:
orange slices   watercress to garnish

Put duck on a board, breast side down. With a sharp knife, cut through the back skin to the back bone. Carefully work the flesh away from the carcass, pressing the knife against the carcass and taking all the meat away from the bone with the skin. Be careful not to split the skin. Remove bones from legs and wings by scraping the flesh from the bones. Leave drumstick bones in place. Remove any excess fat from boned duck and sprinkle with salt and pepper. Fry onion in butter for 5 minutes. Mince chicken livers, pork and liver from the duck. Mix with onion, breadcrumbs, grated rind of 1 orange, herbs and seasoning. Bind with egg. Lay half the stuffing down the centre of the duck. Peel oranges, removing all the white pith, cut in half lengthways. Lay oranges along centre of duck on top of stuffing with cut side uppermost. Cover with remaining stuffing. Fold in ends of duck and draw sides together. Sew with fine string and push into a good shape.

To freeze: Place in a polythene bag, seal and freeze.

To serve: Allow to thaw at room temperature for 8 hours or 24 hours in a refrigerator. Place in roasting tin and roast in a moderately hot oven, for 1½ hours, lowering heat if duck becomes too brown. Serve with orange slices and garnished with watercress. See colour photograph on page 56.

Note: Use duck giblets and bones to make stock (see recipe for Chicken Stock, page 22). Serve duck with gravy made from the stock. Do not store in freezer for more than 1 month.

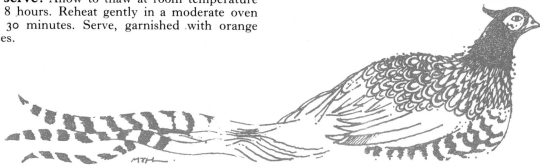

Peach band

Pre-cooking time and oven temperature
20 minutes at 425°F., Gas Mark 7

You will need for 6–8 servings:

6 oz. puff pastry (see page 51) or 1 packet frozen puff pastry (13 oz. size)	1 oz. butter
	few drops vanilla essence
	1 can peach slices
	(1 lb. 13 oz. size)
2 eggs, beaten	1 teaspoon arrowroot
1 oz. flour	1 oz. flaked almonds,
2 oz. castor sugar	browned
½ pint milk	

Roll out pastry and cut into a rectangle, 13 inches by 9 inches. From the long side, cut off two 1-inch strips and do the same from the short side, leaving a rectangle 11 inches by 7 inches. Place on a wet tray. Mix 1 tablespoon of the beaten egg with 1 tablespoon water. Brush edges of pastry with this and place strips round the edge to form a frame. Trim the corners and mitre, like a picture frame. Seal joins well. Knock up edges, using the back of a knife. Brush with egg mixture; bake in a hot oven for 20 minutes or until pastry is risen and golden. Cool. Beat flour into eggs with sugar. Bring milk to the boil and pour over egg mixture, stirring. Return to heat and bring to the boil, stirring all the time until mixture bubbles and thickens. Remove from heat and stir in butter and vanilla essence. Cover with damp greaseproof paper and allow to cool. Drain peaches, reserving ¼ pint of the juice for the glaze. Blend arrowroot with 1 tablespoon of this juice and bring remainder to the boil. Pour over arrowroot, stirring. Return to heat and bring to the boil, stirring all the time until clear. Allow to cool, but not set.
To freeze: Place cooked flan on a piece of double thickness foil. Spread cold pastry cream over the base and top with peaches. Spoon over glaze and sprinkle with almonds. Seal and freeze.
To serve: Allow to thaw at room temperature for 6 hours.

Pineapple meringue shortcake

Pre-cooking time and oven temperature
20 minutes at 375°F., Gas Mark 5 then
30 minutes at 275°F., Gas Mark 1

You will need for 6 servings:

10 oz. plain flour	2 eggs, separated
¼ teaspoon salt	½ oz. flaked almonds
5 oz. butter	(optional)
7 oz. castor sugar	

To serve:

¼ pint double cream	16 oz. can pineapple cubes

Sieve together flour and salt. Rub in butter until mixture resembles fine breadcrumbs, then add 3 oz. of sugar. Blend egg yolks together, add to the flour and mix to a stiff dough. Knead lightly until smooth. Roll out, on a baking sheet, into a circle about ½-inch thick and cut out a 10-inch round. Mark into 6 portions and prick with a fork. Bake in a moderately hot oven for 20 minutes. Whisk egg whites until stiff and peaky. Whisk in half the remaining sugar, then fold in remainder. Spoon tablespoons of meringue round edge of shortcake. Sprinkle with flaked almonds (if used) and return to cool oven for 30 minutes until meringue is crisp and pale golden. Leave for 10 minutes on baking sheet, then cool on wire rack.
To freeze: Wrap in moisture-vapour-proof paper or double thickness foil. Seal and freeze.
To serve: Allow to thaw at room temperature for 3 hours. Lightly whip ¼ pint double cream and fold in drained pineapple cubes from a 16 oz. can, reserving a few for decoration. Sweeten with a little castor sugar if liked. Turn into case and decorate with remaining fruit. See colour photograph on page 53.
Note: Any well-drained canned fruit can be used as an alternative.

Making sandwiches for the freezer

Closed sandwiches should be wrapped in packs and well sealed in heavy-duty foil or special freezer-wrap paper. Some families find it convenient to freeze them in plastic boxes. Open sandwiches and canapés are better stored in foil trays, covered with sheet foil or moisture-vapour-proof paper. Closed sandwiches require 2–3 hours to thaw out, open sandwiches only 1 hour.
Here is the method for making a large quantity of sandwiches for freezing:

1 Decide which fillings to use and prepare these first. Place in refrigerator until required.
2 Make sure that the butter or margarine for spreading is soft but not oily.
3 Have ready foil, boxes and any other packaging material required, including labels as you may wish to pack different assortments and will soon forget the contents of the various containers.
4 Lightly butter all the bread slices on one side right up to the crust. Cover half the slices with filling, and with a second bread slice. Trim if desired, cutting through a

stack of sandwiches at one stroke with a really sharp knife.

5 Wrap closely, cutting sandwiches intended for young children into small sections.
Seal if necessary although with foil packs and plastic boxes this will be unnecessary. Label.

Suggestions For Sandwich Fillings

Cream cheese and chutney
Cream cheese and chives or chopped spring onion
Cream cheese beaten with liver pâté
Grated Cheddar cheese and pickles or chutney
Liver pâté with chopped onion added
Sliced liver sausage, cooked tongue, chicken, mild-cured ham or corned beef
Sliced cooked sausages with mustard
Sardines, mixed with a little vinegar and pepper
Peanut butter
Meat or yeast extract
Stoned dates, heated gently with a little milk and mashed
Jam

Note: The following ingredients are not suitable for sandwiches which are to be deep frozen: Cooked beetroot, cress, cucumber, hard-boiled or scrambled eggs, lettuce, mayonnaise, tomatoes and watercress.

using convenience foods

Commercially frozen foods are wonderful for meals-in-a-moment, but if served straight from the packet can sometimes be a bit dull. It is worth taking a little extra trouble to "dress up" packet frozen dishes to make them more interesting.

You will find in this chapter a number of recipes which involve combining the ready-prepared food with other ingredients to make a complete meal. Using these recipes as a basis on which to build, you will soon find many variations. Fish Puffs can be filled with frozen smoked haddock, for example. A baked flan case can be filled with a mousse of any flavour, lightly mashed down and blended with fruit and whipped cream. There is only one precaution to observe—do not attempt to re-freeze left-overs of any dishes from this section. In fact, it is unwise to re-freeze any food which has been completely thawed and allowed to stand in a warm atmosphere exposed to bacterial contamination.

Kipper ramekins

Cooking time and oven temperature
15 minutes at 425°F., Gas Mark 7

You will need for 6 servings:

1 packet frozen kipper fillets (6 oz. size)	1 oz. Cheddar cheese, grated
1 oz. butter	2 eggs, separated
½ oz. flour	salt and pepper
¼ pint milk	

Cook kippers according to the instructions on the packet. Skin and mash with kipper juices. Melt butter in a pan, add flour and cook for 1 minute. Remove from heat and gradually stir in milk. Return to heat and bring to the boil stirring all the time until mixture bubbles and thickens.

Remove from heat and add cheese, kipper, egg yolks and seasoning. Stiffly whisk egg whites and fold into kipper mixture. Turn into six ¼ pint ramekin dishes and bake in a hot oven for 15 minutes until well risen and golden brown. Serve immediately as a first course.

Marinated kipper salad

You will need for 4 servings:

12 oz. cooked potatoes	1 packet frozen sweet corn kernels (8 oz. size), cooked
2 sticks celery	
1 red-skinned dessert apple	
4 tablespoons mayonnaise	3 tablespoons French dressing
1 packet frozen kipper fillets (6 oz. size)	

Dice potatoes, celery and cored but unpeeled apple into ½-inch pieces. Blend with mayonnaise and pile in the centre of a serving dish. De-frost kipper fillets, skin and cut into narrow strips. Mix with sweet corn and French dressing. Place on the serving dish round the salad.

Crispy cod balls, Chinese style

Cooking time   20 minutes

You will need for 4 servings:

4 oz. long grain rice	5 tablespoons soft brown sugar
1 good pinch saffron powder	2 teaspoons soy sauce
½ pint water	1 tablespoon cornflour, blended with 3 tablespoons water
salt and pepper	
1 packet frozen peas (4 oz. size)	2-inch piece cucumber, diced
½ pint pineapple juice	1 packet crispy cod balls (7 oz. size)
2 tablespoons distilled malt vinegar	

Cook the rice with the saffron in boiling, salted water for 12–15 minutes. Drain, rinse and keep hot. Cook peas according to the instructions on the packet and add to rice. Put pineapple juice, vinegar, sugar and soy sauce into a pan and heat until the sugar dissolves. Bring to the boil and pour over blended cornflour. Return to heat and bring to the boil, stirring all the time until sauce bubbles and thickens and becomes clear. Stir in cucumber. Cook crispy cod balls according to the instructions on the packet. Place rice on a dish, top with cod balls and pour over sauce.

Melt butter, add onion and fry gently for about 5 minutes, add mushrooms and cook until soft. Stir in parsley and seasoning and allow to cool. Roll out pastry to a rectangle 14 inches by 12 inches and cut into four pieces 7 inches by 6 inches. Place a cod steak in the centre of each and divide mushroom mixture among them. Fold pastry over sealing the ends and edges with a little egg, to enclose the cod steak completely. Place on a baking tray with the sealed edges downwards. Brush with egg and make 2 slits on top. Bake in a hot oven for 30–35 minutes.

Crispy cod curry

Cooking time   25 minutes

You will need for 4 servings:

1½ oz. butter	½ pint chicken stock
1 small onion, finely chopped	1 tomato, skinned and sliced
½ small dessert apple, cored and finely chopped	salt
1 tablespoon curry powder	4 oz. long grain rice
1 oz. flour	1 packet crispy cod balls (7 oz. size)

Melt butter, add onion and apple and fry gently until lightly browned. Stir in curry powder and flour and cook gently for 3 minutes. Remove from heat and gradually stir in stock. Return to heat and bring to the boil, stirring all the time until mixture bubbles and thickens. Add tomato and salt, cover and simmer for 10 minutes. While sauce is cooking, cook the rice in boiling, salted water for about 12 minutes, then cook crispy cod balls according to the directions on the packet. Pile rice in the centre of the dish, top with crispy cod balls and spoon sauce round. Serve at once.

Fish puffs

Cooking time   30–35 minutes
Oven temperature   425°F., Gas Mark 7

You will need for 4 servings:

1 oz. butter	salt and pepper
1 small onion, finely chopped	1 packet frozen puff pastry (13 oz. size)
4 oz. mushrooms, chopped	1 packet cod steaks (14 oz. size)
2 teaspoons chopped parsley	1 egg, beaten

Quick steaklet Stroganoff

Cooking time   15 minutes

You will need for 4 servings:

1½ oz. butter	1 can condensed mushroom soup (6 oz. size)
1 medium sized onion, thinly sliced	1 teaspoon tomato purée
1 packet frozen steaklets (11 oz. size), cut into ¼-inch strips	salt and freshly milled black pepper
	1 carton soured cream

Melt butter in a pan and fry onion until soft, without browning. Add strips of steaklets and cook quickly until lightly browned. Stir in mushroom soup, tomato purée and seasoning. Simmer for 8 minutes. Stir in soured cream and serve at once; do not allow to reboil. Serve with boiled rice.

Beefburger pasties

Cooking time   20–25 minutes
Oven temperature   425°F., Gas Mark 7

You will need for 4 servings:

1 packet frozen puff pastry (13 oz. size)	4 large mushrooms
1 packet frozen beefburgers (8 oz. size – 4 beefburgers)	1 large tomato, cut into 4 slices
	1 egg, beaten

Roll pastry out thinly and cut out 8 rounds slightly larger than the beefburger, using a saucer as a guide. Place a beefburger on each round of pastry, then a slice of tomato and top with a mushroom. Brush edges with egg and cover with another pastry round. Seal edges and knock up with the back of a knife. Brush with egg and place on a baking tray. Bake in a hot oven for 20–25 minutes.

Chocolate banana pie

You will need for 6 servings:

1 sponge flan case
  (see page 45)
1 chocolate mousse
  (11 oz. size)

$\frac{1}{4}$ pint double cream,
  lightly whipped
2 bananas, sliced

If using frozen flan case allow it to thaw at room temperature for $1\frac{1}{2}$ hours. Mash mousse and combine with half the cream. Fold in bananas and turn into flan case. Decorate with remaining cream.

Lemon cream flan

You will need for 4 servings:
Biscuit crust:

2 oz. butter
4 oz. digestive biscuits,
  crushed with a rolling pin

1 oz. castor sugar

Filling:

1 lemon mousse
  (11 oz. size)
$\frac{1}{4}$ pint double cream,
  lightly whipped

juice 1 lemon
1 chocolate flake

Melt butter and stir in biscuits and sugar. Mix well. Press biscuit mixture into a loose bottomed 7-inch sandwich tin with a spoon. Leave in refrigerator to set. Mash lemon mousse and combine with cream. Stir in lemon juice. Turn into prepared flan case and chill. Decorate with crumbled chocolate flakes. See the photograph below.

Lemon cream flan

Mousse Alaska

Cooking time   3–5 minutes
Oven temperature   425°F., Gas Mark 7

You will need for 6 servings:

1 sponge flan case
  (see page 45)
1 packet frozen
  strawberries (8 oz. size),
  semi-thawed with a
  little sugar
1 strawberry mousse
  (11 oz. size)

3 egg whites
4 oz. castor sugar, plus
  little extra for dredging
glacé cherries
angelica

Place sponge flan on an ovenproof plate or dish and prick well with a fork. Pour over a little of the juice from the drained fruit. Place mousse in the centre and surround with strawberries. Whisk egg whites until stiff and peaky, gradually whisk in half the 4 oz. of sugar a teaspoon at a time and fold in remainder. Pile meringue on top of the mousse to cover it completely. Dredge with castor sugar. Place in a hot oven for 3–5 minutes, until meringue is lightly browned. Decorate with glacé cherries and angelica.

Variation:
This dish can be made using frozen raspberries and a raspberry mousse instead of strawberries.

Arctic split

Cooking time   5 minutes

You will need for 5 servings:

1 Arctic Roll
1 large orange, peeled
  and cut into segments
1 egg

2 oz. castor sugar
2 oz. mixed candied peel
1 oz. flaked and toasted
  almonds

Place Arctic Roll on a rectangular, flat serving dish and cut into 5 portions to within $\frac{1}{2}$ inch of the base. Place orange segments between slices. Beat egg and sugar in a bowl over hot water for about 5 minutes until thick and frothy. Remove from heat, cool slightly and stir in mixed peel. Pour sauce over roll and sprinkle with nuts.

Index

ACKNOWLEDGEMENTS

The author and publishers thank the following for their co-operation in supplying pictures for this book.

For colour photographs:

Fruit Producers' Council	Pork chops with pears and apricots	Page 21
	Apple cake	Page 53
New Zealand Lamb Information Bureau	Spring lamb pie	Page 21
	Leek and lamb casserole	Page 33

For black and white photographs:
Birds Eye Frozen Foods: Blackberry and apple turnovers and French apple slice, page 54; **Blue Band Bureau**: Paella, page 4; **Flour Advisory Bureau**: Hot cross buns, page 49; **National Dairy Council**: Chocolate éclairs, page 52; **New Zealand Lamb Information Bureau**: Lamb curry, page 35, Moussaka, page 69; **R. Paterson and Sons Ltd., manufacturers of Camp Coffee and Chicory Essence**: Coffee gâteau, page 46, Coffee whirl cake, page 47; **Pyrosil Ware**: French onion soup, page 66; **Bacofoil** for assisting with wrapping and sealing techniques.

USEFUL BOOKS TO READ

There are many books available on freezing techniques plus methods of packing and length of storage. Here is a useful list to consult:

ALL ABOUT HOME FREEZING by Audrey Ellis, Hamlyn. 50p
A COMPREHENSIVE GUIDE TO DEEP FREEZING by Morag Williams, Hamlyn. 30p
DEEP FREEZING by Pat M. Cox, Faber. £4.20p
FOOD FREEZING AT HOME by Gwen Conacher, obtainable from The Electricity Council, Trafalgar Buildings, 1 Charing Cross, London, S.W.1. 20p
MEAL PLANNING WITH YOUR DEEP FREEZE by Kathleen Thomas, Hamlyn. 30p
MEALS TO ENJOY FROM YOUR FREEZER by Audrey Ellis, Hamlyn. 50p
STEP BY STEP GUIDE TO HOME FREEZING by Audrey Ellis, Hamlyn. 80p

© The Hamlyn Publishing Group Limited 1970
ISBN 0 600 01360 X
Published by The Hamlyn Publishing Group Limited
London · New York · Sydney · Toronto
Hamlyn House, Feltham, Middlesex, England
First published 1970. Third impression 1972
Printed in England by Fleetway Printers, Gravesend, Kent